MS Excel

MS Excel

Let's Advance to The Next Level

Anurag Singal

BEP BUSINESS EXPERT PRESS

MS Excel: Let's Advance to The Next Level

First published in 2017 by
Business Expert Press, LLC
222 East 46th Street, New York, NY 10017
www.businessexpertpress.com

ISBN-13: 978-1-63157-943-1 (paperback)
ISBN-13: 978-1-63157-944-8 (e-book)

Business Expert Press Quantitative Approaches to Decision Making Collection

Collection ISSN: 2163-9515 (print)
Collection ISSN: 2163-9582 (electronic)

Cover and interior design by Exeter Premedia Services Private Ltd., Chennai, India

First edition: 2017

10 9 8 7 6 5 4 3 2 1

Printed in the United States of America.

Abstract

'MS Excel—Let's advance to the Next Level' is an attempt to take you to the next orbit of competence in this fascinating world. It is a ready reckoner for any practitioner who seeks to further his/her understanding of the tools and utilities. MS Excel offers to make life easier for a data analyst. Thus, it will be of relevance to students, academicians, the ones pursuing corporate careers as well as entrepreneurs preparing business plans for their startups.

The book explains a wide array of complex functions, ranging from V-LOOKUP to MATCH/INDEX and Pivot Tables in very practical, simple, and implementable manner. Also the segments on Conditional Formatting and printing tricks will help you better present the output to stakeholders. Do try the features Excel has on offer for controlling data input as well as creating checks and balances to ensure cell/sheet/file-level security.

You will get the most out of this book if you can use this as a workbook and simultaneously practice the functions on the computer. It is for this purpose that we have appended screenshots for each function. Take each function as a mini case study and try to analyze how you can apply it in making more sense of the enormous data at your disposal.

Once you are through all the modules, I am sure, you will emerge as a more efficient person on the work-front.

Keywords

Advanced Excel Formulas, Big Data processing, Microsoft Excel Basics, Microsoft Excel Latest Version, Microsoft Office Excel Worksheet, Microsoft Office, MS Excel Keyboard Shortcuts, MS Excel

Contents

Preface

The operational efficiency of any knowledge professional can improve significantly with an upgradation of his or her skills of MS Excel. With every additional function that you learn, life can become a lot easier.

This books aims to simplify things. It will take you from the basics and if all goes well, you shall be able to move to the next level of MS Excel by the time you reach the end.

Don't just read this book like a novel. Practice it and the learning curve will be the steepest.

"The proof of the pudding lies in the eating." So let the pages make their sales pitch themselves.

Anurag Singal graduated from IIM A PGPX in the year 2015. He can be reached at x14anurag@iima.ac.in.

#0101–0109: *Super Essential Keyboard Shortcuts*

Starters		
1	Alt	Press and release the ALT key to display the *Key Tips* next to each Ribbon command
2	Ctrl C; Ctrl X; Ctrl V	Copy; Cut; Paste
3	Ctrl D	Copies the cell contents down
4	Ctrl R	Copies the cell contents to the right
5	Ctrl Enter	To fill all the selected cells with text/nos./formula
Workbook Navigation		
6	Ctrl PgDn	Moves to the next sheet
7	Ctrl PgUp	Moves to the previous sheet
Sheet Navigation and Cell(s) Selection		
8	Ctrl A	Selects the entire worksheet/data array depending on active cell selected
9	Ctrl Arrow key	Moves to the edge of a data block; if the cell is blank, moves to the first nonblank cell
10	Shift Arrow key	Expands the selection in the direction indicated (one cell at a time)
11	Ctrl Shift Arrow key	Select from the active cell to the end of a row/column
12	Ctrl Shift End key	Selects from the active cell to the last used cell
13	Ctrl BackSpace	Navigate to the beginning of selected data (keeping the selection intact)
14	Shift Spacebar	Selects the entire row(s) in the selected range
15	Ctrl Spacebar	Selects the entire column(s) in the selected range
Row/Column—Add or Delete		
16	Alt I C	Insert Column
17	Alt I R	Insert Row
18	Ctrl Shift +	Displays the Insert dialog box to insert new cells/rows/columns
19	Ctrl −	Displays the Delete dialog box to delete the selected cells/rows/columns
Formula		
20	F4	Repeats the last command or action, if possible
21	F4	Also, used for Cell referencing ($); discussed later
22	F2	Begins editing the active cell

23	Ctrl `	Displays the formula in each cell instead of the resulting value [Hint: ` is back tick key above the TAB key]
24	Ctrl [and F5+Enter	Navigate to precedent cells and return back [*conditions apply]
25	ALT =	Auto sum
26	Ctrl A after formula open	Opens up "Function Arguments" box. For example, after writing =SUM(, press Ctrl A
27	Shift F3	Call out "Insert Function (fx)"/"Function Arguments" dialog box
28	Tab and Shift Tab	Moves down/up among a series of tabs/boxes
Format		
29	Ctrl 1	Activates "Format cells"
30	Ctrl;	Inserts today's date
31	Ctrl Shift 3	Changes the date format to "22-May-2015"
32	Alt H K	Applies the Number format with two decimal places, thousands separator, and minus sign (−) for negative values
Miscl		
33	Ctrl F2	Print Preview
34	Ctrl F1	Displays or hides the ribbon
35	Alt;	Selects visible cell from the selection
Paste Special		
36	Alt, E, S, V ENTER	Paste Special – Value
37	Ctrl Alt V V Enter	
38	QAT	

#0201: *Used in Financial Modeling and Tax Computation*

=MAX(_{MAX(number1, [number2], ...)}	• Used in **Tax Computations and Financial Models to prevent choosing of negative numbers** for subsequent calculations. • For example, =MAX(0,A1) chooses 0 or value in cell A1, whichever is higher • For example, penalty for late deposit = higher of 2% of dues or Rs.100
=MIN(_{MIN(number1, [number2], ...)}	• Used in logics such as lower of the two numbers in the area of **Tax Computations,** specific areas of **Financial Engineering** § =MIN(A1:A5) is same as =SMALL(A1:A5,1)

#0202: *Used in Pricing Discovery Processes*

=LARGE(_{LARGE(array, k)}	• **Auction** such as highest bid value, second highest bid value and so on. For example, H2 will be =LARGE(A1:A5,2)
=SMALL(_{SMALL(array, k)}	• **Vendor evaluation** such as lowest bid value L1, second lowest bid value L2 and so on. For example, L2 will be =SMALL(A1:A5,2)

#0203–0204: *For Rounding Numbers*

=ROUND(_{ROUND(number, num_digits)}	• "*num_digits*" signifies "number of decimal digits." For example, for the starting number • 52.233 – "2" implies 52.23, "1" implies 52.20, and 0 implies 52.00 • **=ROUND(A1/50, 0) * 50** [implies nearest 50]—same technique **also applicable with ROUNDUP and ROUNDDOWN** • For example, Cell A1 = 5344.2 • =ROUND(A1/10,0)*10 = 5340.0
=ROUNDDOWN(_{ROUNDDOWN(number, num_digits)}	• For example, Cell A1 = 5349.2 • =ROUNDDOWN(A1/10,0)*10 = 5340.0
=ROUNDUP(_{ROUNDUP(number, num_digits)}	• For example, Cell A1 = 5342.2 • =ROUNDUP(A1/10,0)*10 = 5350.0
• § MROUND() do not work with +/– numbers simultaneously AND it does not accommodate the logic of round up and round down.	

#0205: *For Counting*

=COUNT(_{COUNT(value1, [value2], ...)}	• Counts the number of cells which have numeric value.
=COUNTA(_{COUNTA(value1, [value2], ...)}	• Counts the number of cells which IS NOT a blank (i.e., numbers, alphabets, alphanumeric, space).
=COUNTBLANK(_{COUNTBLANK(range)}	• Counts the number of cells which IS a blank.
• COUNTIF() and COUNTIFS() will be discussed later in the book. COUNTIFS() is a logic-based cell counting mechanism.	

#0206–0207: *For Weighted Average and Compounding/Discounting*

=SUMPRODUCT(_{SUMPRODUCT(array1, [array2], [array3], ...)}	• Multiplies corresponding cells in **two or more ranges** and returns the sum of those products. For example, =SUMPRODUCT(A1:A2,B1:B2) = (A1*B1) + (A2*B2) § The array arguments must have the **same dimensions.** For example, =SUMPRODUCT(A1:A2,B1:<u>B3</u>) is invalid. • Used with =SUM() for computing **weighted average.** • Was used to create condition-based sum logic before SUMIFS() was introduced.
=POWER(_{POWER(number, power)}	• Used in Financial Modeling—discounting cash flows, compounding. • Caret sign ($\wedge$) is a perfect substitute. For example, 25 =POWER(5,2) and is same as =5$\wedge$2.

#0301–0302: Formatting Tricks Incl. Special Custom Formats
[Shortcut: Ctrl 1]

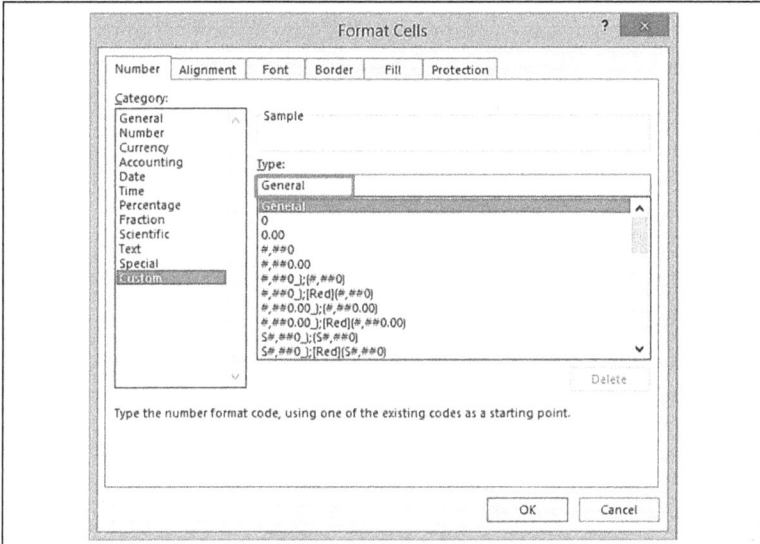

CUSTOM FORMAT	EFFECT
@*.	"Cell width adjusted" trailing full stops
"Rs."	Prefix/Suffix
000000	Self-adjusting Prefix Zeroes (up to 6)

- "Double-click" Format Painter to use it uninterruptedly. Press <Esc> to return escape out of Format Painter mode.

#0303–#0304: *Using CELL STYLES for Automating Formatting for MIS Reporting and Financial Models*

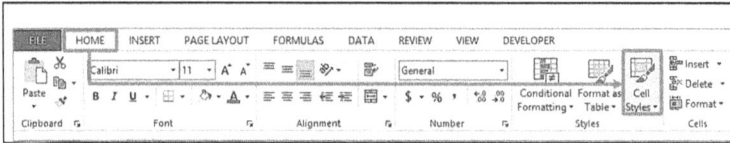

"**New Cell Style**" lets you create customized cell format which you can apply and reapply on any worksheet of the workbook. Additionally, if you change the "definition" of any existing cell style, the changes are universal. Thus, **modifying a cell style affects all cells in a workbook that use that cell style**. This can save a lot of time.

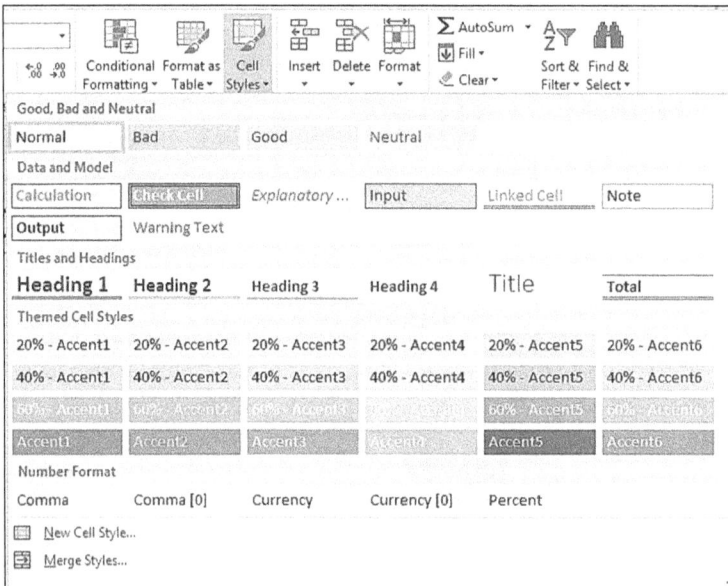

- Right click a cell style to modify or delete it.
- A cell style is stored in the workbook where you create it.
- Open a new workbook and click on "**Merge Styles**" (beneath New Cell Style) to import a cell style (keep the old workbook with the original cell style <u>open</u>).

#0305–#0307: Cell Drag–n–Drop Auto Fill Options

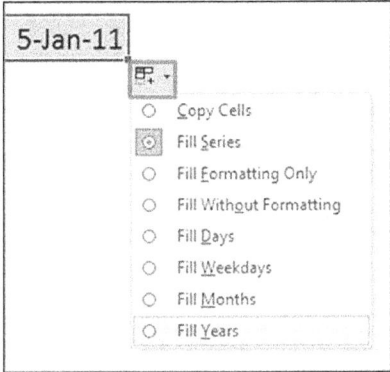

- Also, refer =EOMONTH() for formula-based Fill Months (1), Fill Quarters (3) and Fill Years (12)
- If the fill–handle doesn't appear or the mouse cursor isn't allowing you to draw the contents of a cell, please check if the "**Enable fill handle and cell drag–and–drop**" setting is turned ON.

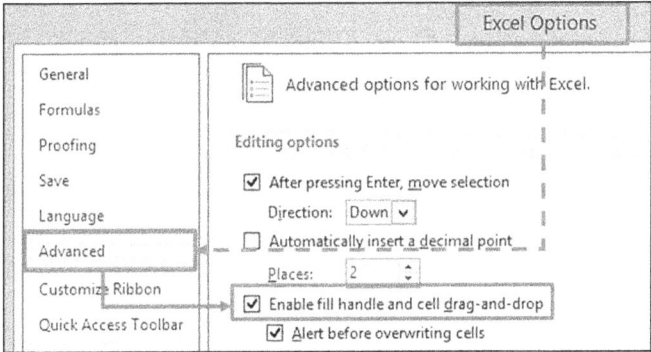

#0308 Paste Special—Transpose vs. TRANSPOSE()

- **Paste Special—Transpose** switches/rearranges the data in a table from rows and columns to columns and rows, respectively. However, it doesn't create "links" to the original cells. Thus, any change in the original table will not affect the "transposed" table.
- Writing a **=TRANSPOSE() formula** with **Ctrl + Shift + Enter** will create links too o Copy the dataset to be "transposed" o Paste Special—Transpose.
  - o <Delete> cell values but keep the cell selection intact (this is to avoid counting the original cells and carefully select a fresh range in line with that).
  - o Directly type **=TRANSPOSE(** and then, choose the original range of data, say A1:B5.
  - o Close the parentheses ")" and press Ctrl + Shift + Enter together to enter the formula as an "array" formula.

#0401—0402: Absolute and Relative Referencing Using $ (Locking the Cell/Range)

- After selecting a cell or a range of cells, keep pressing the function key **<F4>** to toggle between the four combinations of cell referencing (as indicated):

=A1	=$A$1
–	Row Fixed&Col Fixed
A1 becomes B1 if copied **sideways (right)**	$A$1 remains $A$1 if copied **sideways**
A1 becomes A2 if copied **downwards**	$A$1 remains $A$1 if copied **downwards**

=A$1	=$A1
Row Fixed	Col Fixed
A$1 becomes B$1 if copied **sideways (right)**	$A1 remains $A1 if copied **sideways**
A$1 remains A$1 if copied **downwards**	$A1 becomes $A2 if copied **downwards**

#0501–0506: *Go To—Special (Ctrl + G or F5)*

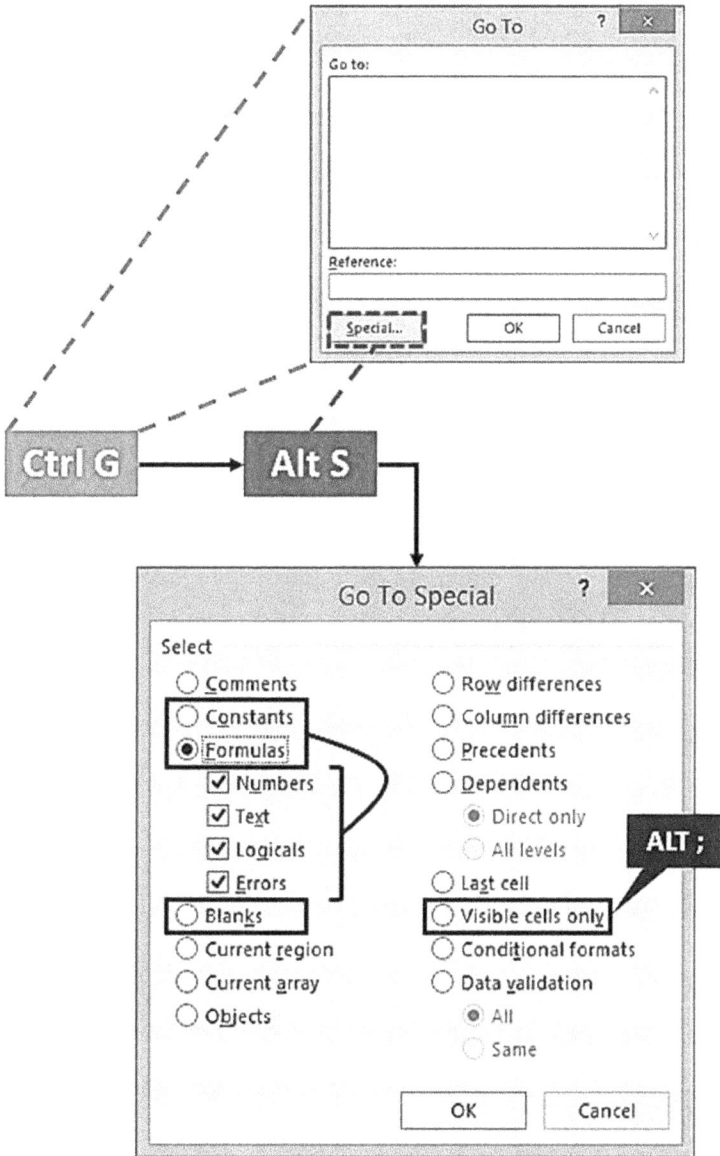

- Often used with **Ctrl+Enter**: With multiple cells selected (can be noncontiguous), this shortcut will enter the same data/ formula logic in all cells in the selection at once.

#0601 *Vertical Sort—1-Level and 2-Level*

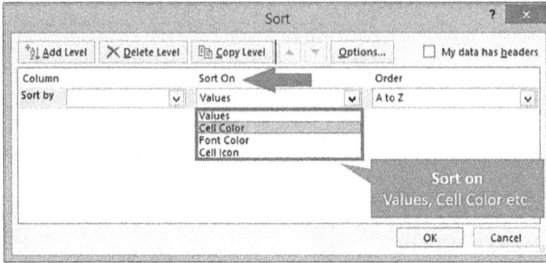

#0602: *Custom Sorting*

- **"Order" > "Custom":** allows to prepare own custom sequence in which the data can be sorted. For example, Partner, Director, Sr Manager, Manager, Analyst <u>OR</u> North, East, West, South.

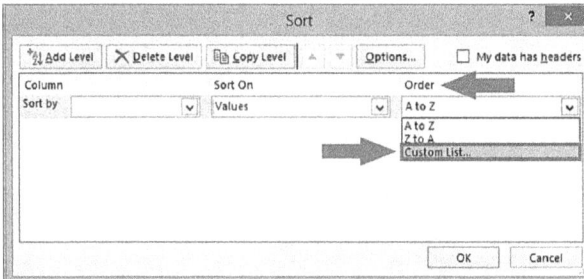

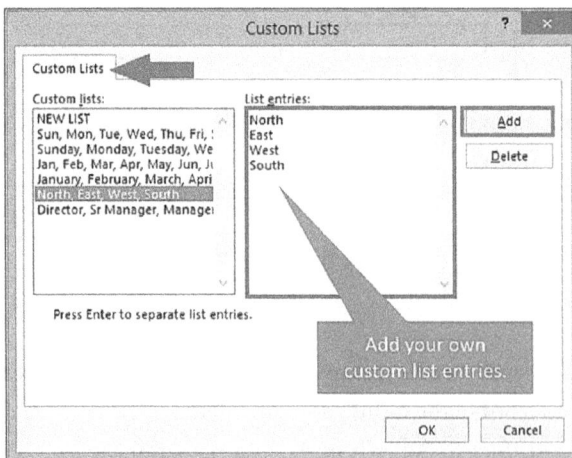

#0603 Sort Trick—Add Alternate Blank Rows In-Between Existing Rows

	A	B	C	D	E	F	G	H
1	Zone	Amt. $	DUMMY SN			Zone	Amt. $	DUMMY SN
2	North	1,612	1			North	1,612	1
3	North	285	2					1
4	North	611	3			North	285	2
5	East	501	4					2
6	East	241	5			North	611	3
7	West	586	6					3
8	West	1,213	7			East	501	4
9	West	374	8					4
10	South	9,321	9		S	East	241	5
11	South	324	10		O			5
12	South	2,775	11		R	West	586	6
13	South	1,954	12		T			6
14			1			West	1,213	7
15			2					7
16			3			West	374	8
17			4					8
18			5			South	9,321	9
19			6					9
20			7			South	324	10
21			8					10
22			9			South	2,775	11
23			10					11
24			11			South	1,954	12
25			12					12

#0604: *Horizontal Sorting (Left to Right)*

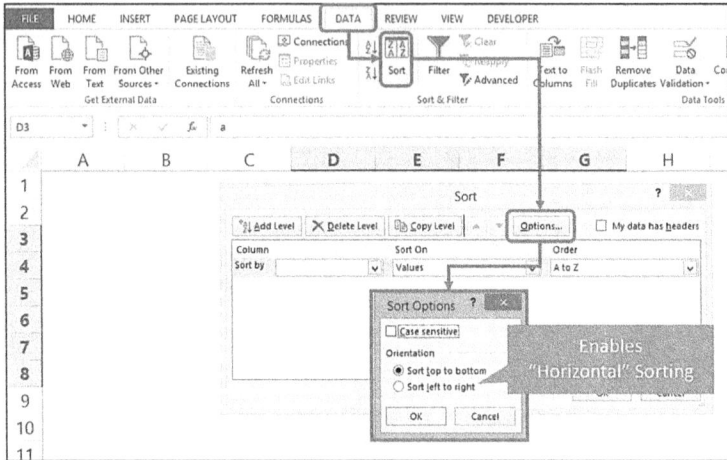

- **"Options" > "Horizontal Sort > Left to Right":** is used to rearrange the columns—all at once, without using "Cut" and "Insert Cut Cells" for each instance.
- Using **synthetic "DUMMY Serial No."** column helps (1) create blank rows in-between and, (2) remember the original sequence of row items.

#0605–0606: Filter—Choosing the Dataset Correctly

- Choosing just the header row/cells before applying Filter will lead the "Filter" to ignore the data rows after the blank row.

#0607: *Filter Analysis w. Shortcuts*

1.	Alt, A, T	Apply/Deactivate Filter on selected dataset.
2.	Alt + down-arrow	To open up the Filter drop-down options from the header row.
3.	Spacebar	To check ON/OFF square checkbox.
4.	Home	To quickly reach to the beginning of the options in list of square checkboxes Used to "Select All," which is placed at the beginning of the list.
5.	End	To quickly reach to the end of the options in list of square checkboxes. Used to navigate to the "(Blank)" or "#N/A" option, which are placed at the bottom of the list.
6.	Alt =	For example, to generate a =SUBTOTAL(9,$C$2:$C$200) formula for AutoSum.

#0608–0609: *Using =SUBTOTAL() for Calculations w. Filtered List*

- In filtered lists, SUBTOTAL() always ignores values in hidden rows, regardless of *function_num*. For example, 1 for AVERAGE, 9 for SUM, 109 for SUM again.

- In tables with Filter applied, SUB-OTAL() with 109 that is, SUM will ignore values in the manually hidden rows whereas SUBOTAL() with 9 will not.

- Shortcut for SUBTOTAL() formula for autosum in filtered lists is **ALT =**

#0610: Filter—Applying 2 or More Filters Simultaneously on the Same Sheet

- Creating two (or more) distinct Filtered list on the same sheet is not possible through "Data" tab > "Filter." Instead, use "Insert" tab > "Table" (or Ctrl + T)

#0611: Filter—Color Filter and Text Filter

#0612–0614: *Advanced Filter*

- Advanced Filter can simultaneously pick up differential criteria unlike Filter. For example, list of clients from Park Plaza with amount >70,000 AND from Shantiniketan" with amount ">50,000" has to be extracted in one go.

Criteria	Records selected...
P	Starts with the character- P
Park	Starts with the word- Park
="=P"	Only contains the character- P
'=P	Only contains the character- P
="=Park"	Only contains the text- Park
'=Park	Only contains the text- Park
="=S?N"	Contains text that begins with S, has one character, and then the letter N (may be more than three characters long)
'=S?N	Contains text that begins with S, has one character, and then the letter N (may be more than 3 characters long)
="=S*N"	Contains text that begins with S, has one or more other characters, and then the letter N
'=S*N	Contains text that begins with S, has one or more other characters, and then the letter N

=	Contains a blank
<>	Contains a nonblank entry
<>A*	Contains any text except text that begins with A
<>*A	Contains any text except text that ends with A
'=???	Contains exactly three characters
<>????	Does not contain exactly four characters

Note: Text filters are not Case Sensitive

#0701–0702: *Every Valid Date (i.e., Date That Can Be Understood by Excel) Is a Number*

- 2-Jan-1900 is 2 days away from 31-Dec-1899 and hence, read by Excel as 2.0.
- Use =**ISNUMBER**() to detect validity of Dates entered that is, whether the displayed date is a number.
- Use **"Format Cells" or Ctrl + 1** to change the **"skin"** or the display value of the date
  - Use "*Comma Style*" or "General" to display the number
  - **Ctrl + Shift + 3** will convert a correct date's display value to dd-mm-yyyy format or 22-Jul-2015.
- Microsoft OS: **Control Panel > Region & Language > Settings**—to change the format of the date input accepted by Excel

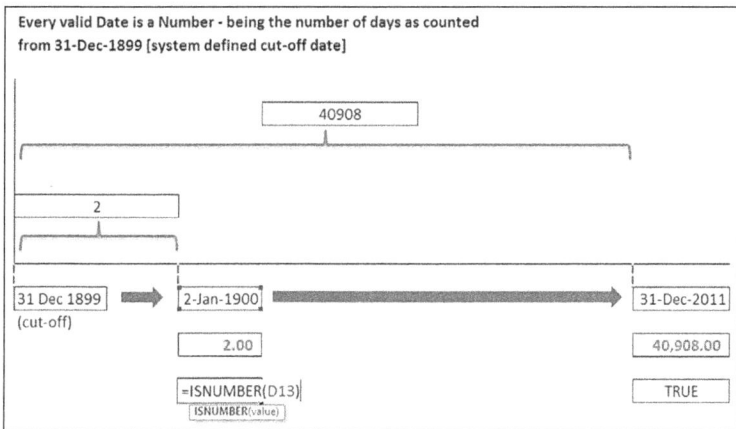

Every valid Date is a Number - being the number of days as counted from 31-Dec-1899 [system defined cut-off date]

40908

2

31 Dec 1899 (cut-off)	2-Jan-1900	31-Dec-2011
	2.00	40,908.00
	=ISNUMBER(D13)	TRUE
	ISNUMBER(value)	

#0703: *Extracting Date Information Through Formulas—DAY(),*
MONTH(), YEAR(), DATE()

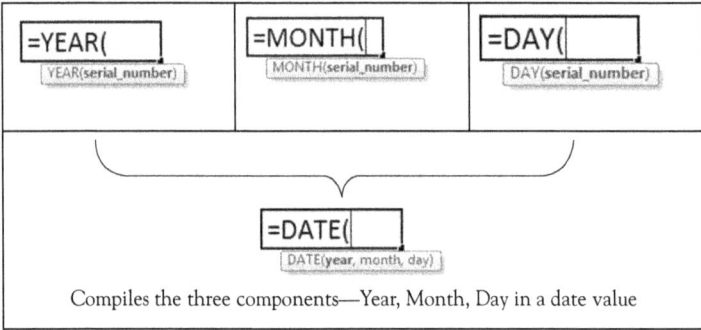

	A	B	C	D	E	F	G
1							
2			=DAY()	=MONTH()	=YEAR()		=DATE()
3	3-Jun-11		3	6	2011		3-Jun-11
4							
5			=DAY(A3)	=MONTH(A3)	=YEAR(A3)		=DATE(E3,D3,C3)

=YEAR(
YEAR(serial_number)

=MONTH(
MONTH(serial_number)

=DAY(
DAY(serial_number)

=DATE(
DATE(year, month, day)

Compiles the three components—Year, Month, Day in a date value

#0704: *Extracting Date Information*

- Converts the date into Custom format. For example, "mmmm-yyyy" will display June-2011.
- Important: Resultant answer value is not a date value but a text value. Used for display purposes and not for subsequent formula computations.

	A	B	C	D	E
1					
2			**=TEXT()**		
3	3-Jun-11		Friday		=TEXT(A3,"dddd")
4	3-Jun-11		Fri		=TEXT(A3,"ddd")
5	3-Jun-11		03		=TEXT(A3,"dd")
6					
7			**=TEXT()**		
8	3-Jun-11		June		=TEXT(A8,"mmmm")
9	3-Jun-11		Jun		=TEXT(A9,"mmm")
10	3-Jun-11		06		=TEXT(A10,"mm")
11					
12					
13			**=TEXT()**		
14	3-Jun-11		2011		=TEXT(A14,"yyyy")
15	3-Jun-11		2011		=TEXT(A15,"yyy")
16	3-Jun-11		11		=TEXT(A16,"yy")

#0705: Date Formulas—WEEKDAY(), WORKDAY(), NETWORKDAYS()

=WEEKDAY(<small>WEEKDAY(serial_number, [return_type])</small>	▪ Returns a value from 1 to 7, representing day of the week. ▪ For example, 1 = Sunday, 2 = Monday, 7 = Saturday. ▪ Used with IF() to write day-based logical formula. For example, *=IF(WEEKDAY(A1)=1,"Holiday,""Office Day")* ▪ Scheduled public holidays can also be excluded.
=WORKDAY(<small>WORKDAY(start_date, days, [holidays])</small>	▪ Returns the date before or after a specified number of weekdays (weekends excluded). It **excludes start date** in computing final answer. ▪ For example, if Cell A1 is 30-Dec-2011, then *=WORK-DAY(A7,5)-1* will return 5-Jan-2012. 1-Jan-2012 is a Sunday and hence, excluded. ▪ Scheduled public holidays can also be excluded. ▪ Used to calculate deadline/due date calculations.
=NETWORKDAYS(<small>NETWORKDAYS(start_date, end_date, [holidays])</small>	▪ Returns the number of weekdays (weekends excluded) between two dates. ▪ It **includes start date** in computing final answer. ▪ Scheduled public holidays can also be excluded. ▪ Used to calculate number of business days between two dates.
▪ WORKDAY.INTL() and NETWORKDAY.INTL() have been introduced from v. 2010 onwards. They incorporate the logic that multiple country may have different weekends. Refer Lecture **#0706-#0707.**	

#0706: WORKDAY.INTL() for Deadline/Due Date Calculations w. Custom Weekends/Holidays

=WORKDAY.INTL(<small>WORKDAY.INTL(start_date, days, [weekend], [holidays])</small>	
Saturday and Sunday are weekend days 1 - Saturday, Sunday 2 - Sunday, Monday 3 - Monday, Tuesday 4 - Tuesday, Wednesday 5 - Wednesday, Thursday 6 - Thursday, Friday 7 - Friday, Saturday 11 - Sunday only 12 - Monday only 13 - Tuesday only 14 - Wednesday only 15 - Thursday only 16 - Friday only 17 - Saturday only	▪ Returns the date before or after a specified number of weekdays (weekends excluded). It **excludes start date** in computing final answer. ▪ Scheduled public holidays can also be excluded. ▪ Used to calculate deadline/due date calculations and in Project Management. ▪ **How is it different from =WORKDAY()?** ▪ Allows the user to specify which days are counted as weekends. ▪ For example, 7 = Fri/Sat are weekends as followed by Saudi Arabia.

#0706: NETWORKDAYS.INTL() for No. of Business Days Calculations w. Custom Weekends/Holidays

=NETWORKDAYS.INTL(
NETWORKDAYS.INTL(start_date, end_date, [weekend], [holidays])

| Saturday and Sunday are weekend days
1 - Saturday, Sunday
2 - Sunday, Monday
3 - Monday, Tuesday
4 - Tuesday, Wednesday
5 - Wednesday, Thursday
6 - Thursday, Friday
7 - Friday, Saturday
11 - Sunday only
12 - Monday only
13 - Tuesday only
14 - Wednesday only
15 - Thursday only
16 - Friday only
17 - Saturday only | • Returns the number of weekdays (weekends excluded) between two dates.
• It **includes start date** in computing final answer.
• Scheduled public holidays can also be excluded.
• Used to calculate number of business days between two dates and in
• Project Management.
• **How is it different from =NETWORK-DAYS()?**
• Allows the user to specify which days are counted as weekends.
• For example, 7 = Fri/Sat are weekends as followed by Saudi Arabia. |

#0708: Date Formulas—TODAY() and NOW() w. Shortcut

=TODAY() TODAY()	• Returns the current date as per PC's system clock. • Updates every time the file is opened (dynamic). • **Ctrl +;** and press **Enter** - for inserting current date (static).
=NOW() NOW()	• Returns the current date and time as per PC's system clock. • Updates every time the file is opened (dynamic). • **Ctrl + Shift +;** and press **Enter** - for inserting current time (static).

#0709: Date Formulas—EOMONTH() for Financial Modeling, Budgets, Due Dates

=EOMONTH(EOMONTH(start_date, months)	• Returns the **last day of the month** before or after a specified number of months. • Used for due dates computations such as 5th of next month, end of current month. • Used for creating timelines in Budget & Forecast models—MoM, QoQ, YoY.

#0710 Date Formulas—EDATE() for Financial Modeling, Budgets, Due Dates

=EDATE(EDATE(start_date, months)	<ul><li>Returns the date that represents the indicated number of months before or after the start date. For example, 60 days vs. 2 months.</li><li>Used for computing 3 months' notice period end date, retirement age, probation period, contract deadline, EMI installment due date.</li></ul>

#0801–0802: Data Validation—Drop Down List and Range Naming

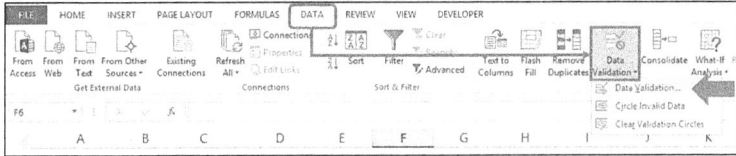

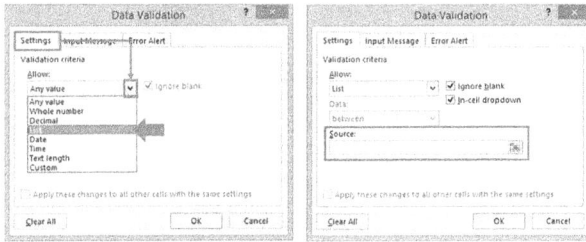

Source: Accepted,Rejected	▪ Hard-coded values separated by comma.
Source: =$A$1:$A$5	▪ Cell range containing input values.
Source: =listname	▪ Named cell range from same/different worksheet. Refer cell/range Naming via-name Box. The prefix = (equal sign) is important here.

Note: (1) =INDIRECT() w. named ranges and (2) =OFFSET() can also be used to create dynamic ranges.

	▪ Name Box – Select cell(s), Write Name, press <Enter>. ▪ NB: <F3> to activate Names List Box.

- **NAME MANAGER:** Cell(s)/Range Naming–Editing/
  Deleting "names"/"referred range"
- **CREATE FROM SELECTION:** for bulk naming

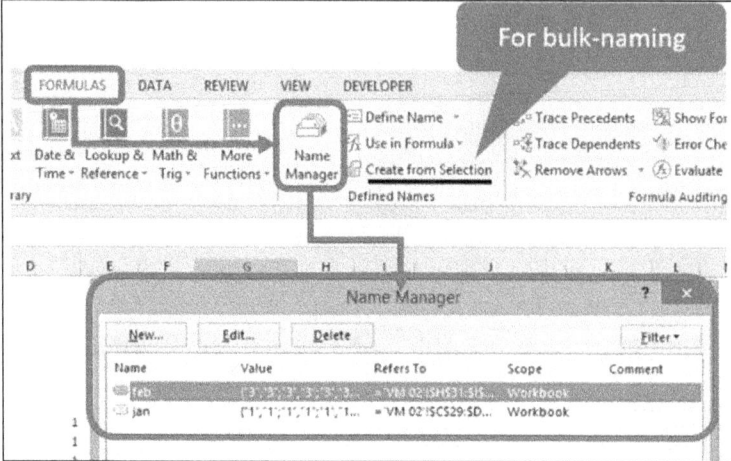

#0803: Data Validation—Numbers w. Error Alert and Input Message

| 1 | Input Message | To display a message when a cell is selected. |
| 2 | Error Alert | To display an alert if invalid data is entered in a cell. |

Sample Output

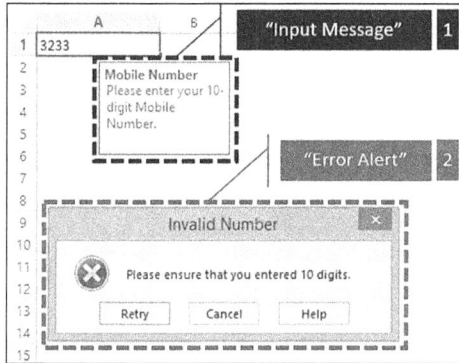

Procedure to activate "Input Message" and "Error Alert"

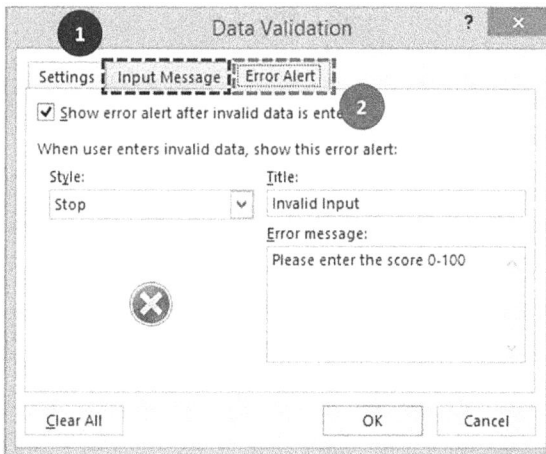

#0804: Data Validation—Dates w. Error Alert and Circle Invalid Data

A cell with predefined data validation logic will accept only those user inputs as validated by the rule. For example, values as per drop-down list.

However, one can mistakenly **supersede** these rules by copying an invalid data from a different cell and use **Paste Special (Value)** on top of the cell with data validation. This procedure allows the cell with data validation to accept the invalid data. So in order to highlight the cells with invalid values, we use "**Circle Invalid Data.**"

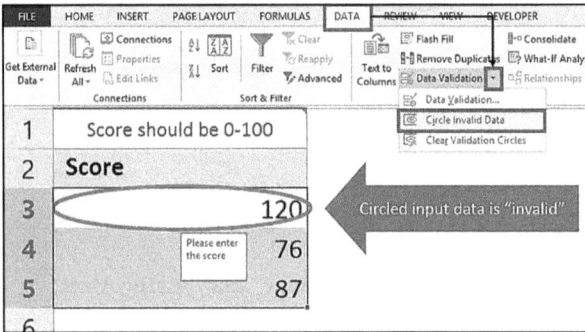

#0805: Data Validation—Whole number, Text Length, Date (MM/DD/YYYY)

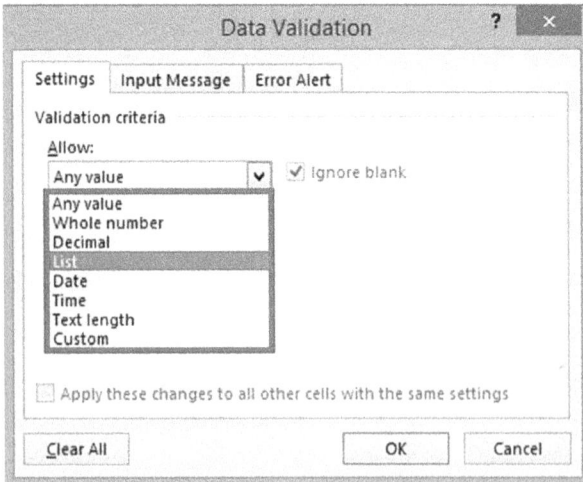

#0806: *Data Validation—Custom w. Formula Logic*

The CUSTOM logic should be famed to yield LOGICAL (True/False) result.

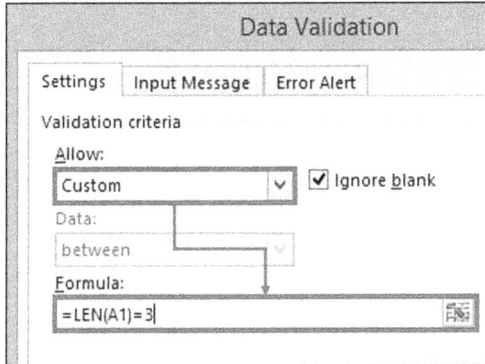

#0901–0902: *Grouping/UnGrouping Columns and Rows*

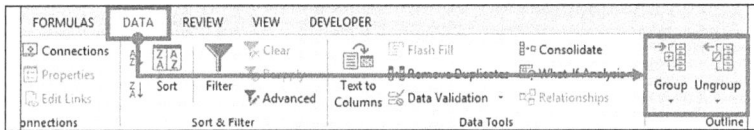

#0903: Grouping Trick: Changing Placement of Grouping Button

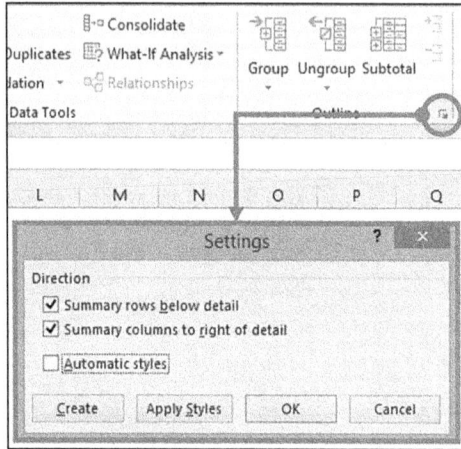

#0904: Cell Gridlines: Turning On/Off

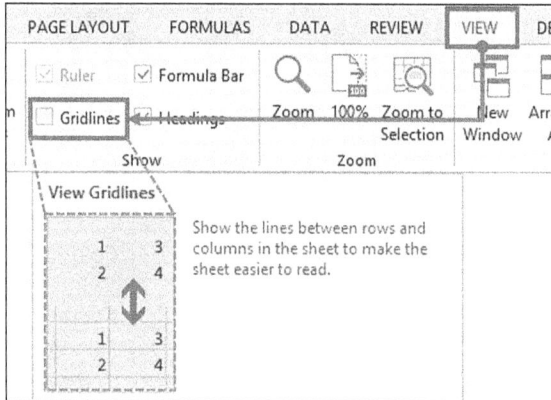

#0905: Hide/Unhide Rows and Columns

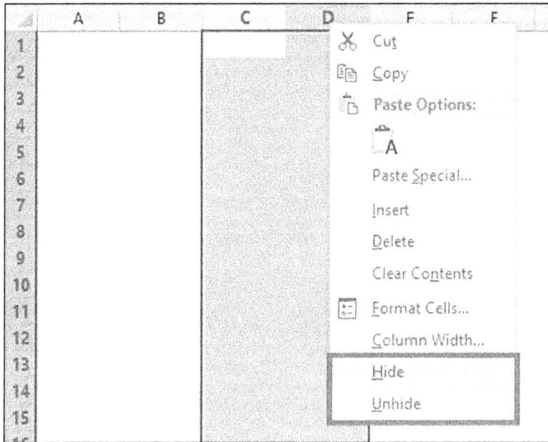

#0906: Freeze Panes (Incl. Both Row and Column Simultaneously)

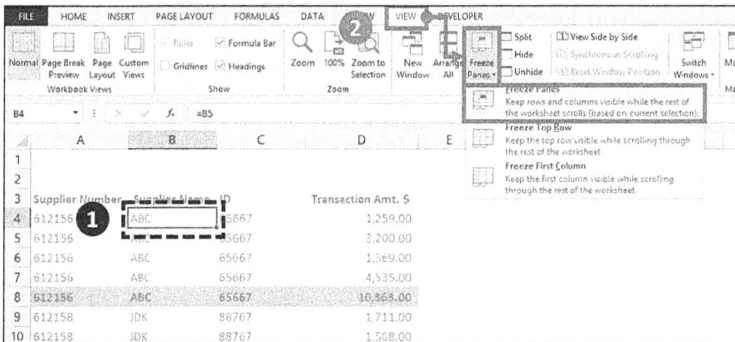

Choose the cell the row above which and the column before which needs to be "frozen." In this case, Column A and Rows 1 to 3 will be frozen.

#1001–1003: Pivot Tables—Prerequisites, How to Create

Prerequisites:
- Blank/Empty "header" cells not allowed.
- "Merged" cells not allowed.

Creating a Pivot Table
- Choose the data table. INSERT > PIVOT TABLE.

Changing an Essential Setting:

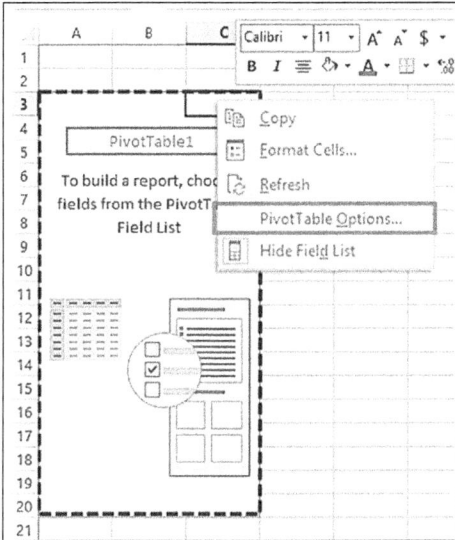

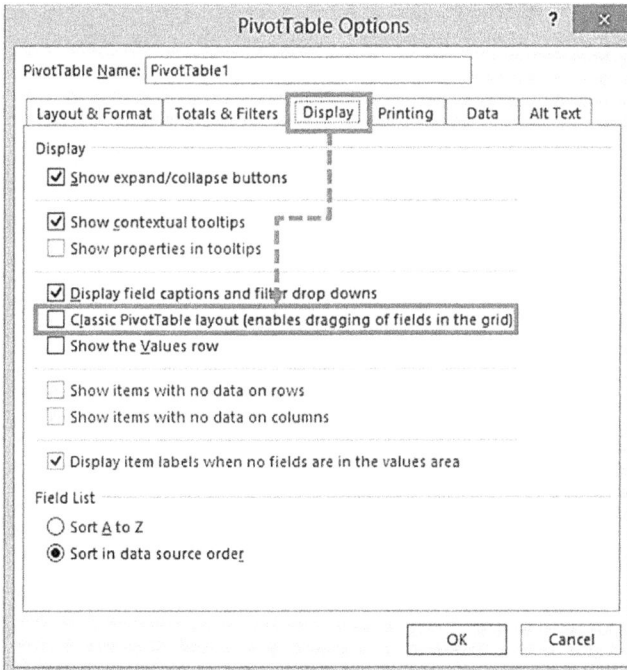

#1004: Pivot Tables—Exploring Pivot Table Grid (Fields)

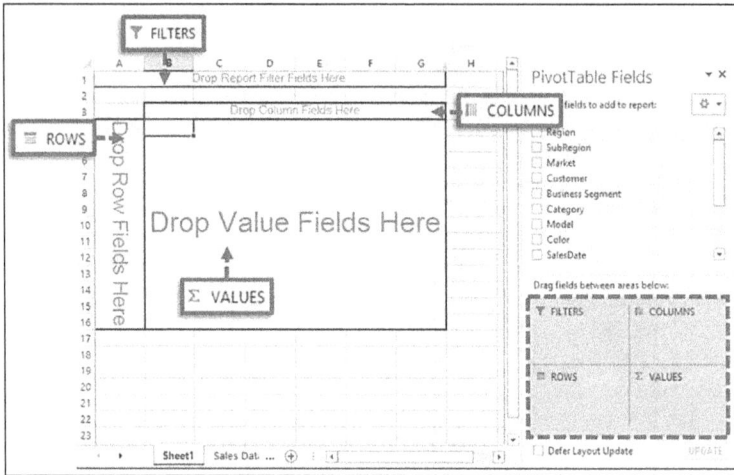

#1005: Pivot Tables—Value Field Settings for Sum, Average

#1006–1007: *Pivot Tables—Value Field Settings for % Calculations*

Calculation	Meaning
1/4	% of Grand Total
1/2	% of Column Total
1/3	% of Row Total

#1008–1009: Pivot Tables—Grouping Dates and Numbers (Automatic)

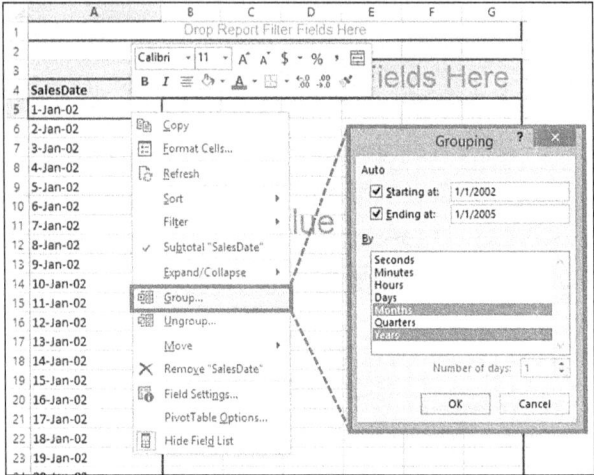

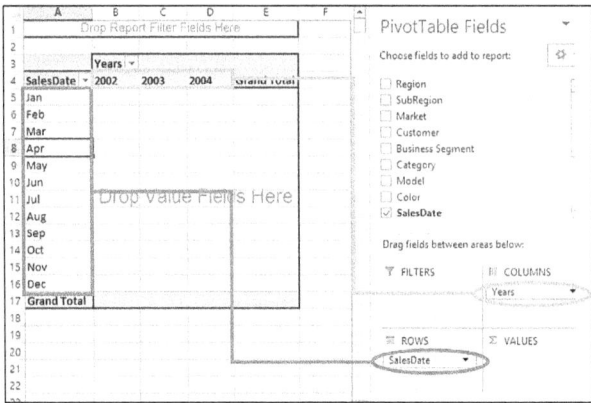

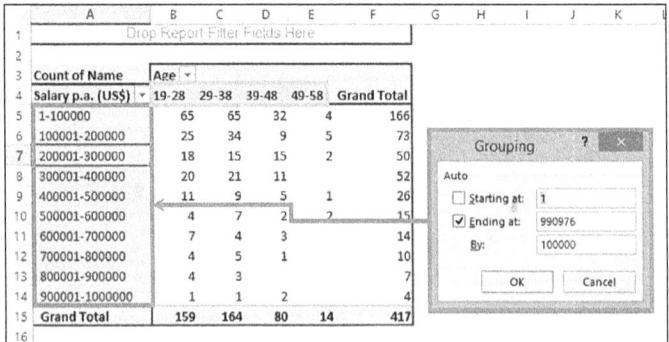

#1010: *Pivot Tables—Grouping Text (Manual)*

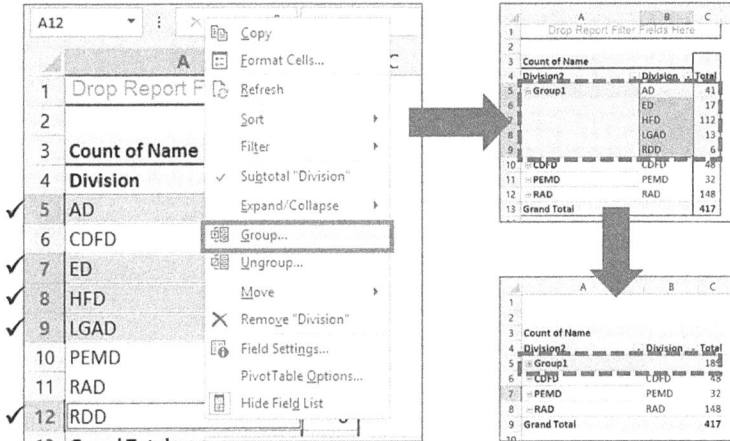

#1011: *Pivot Table—Refresh vs. Refresh All, Change Data Source*

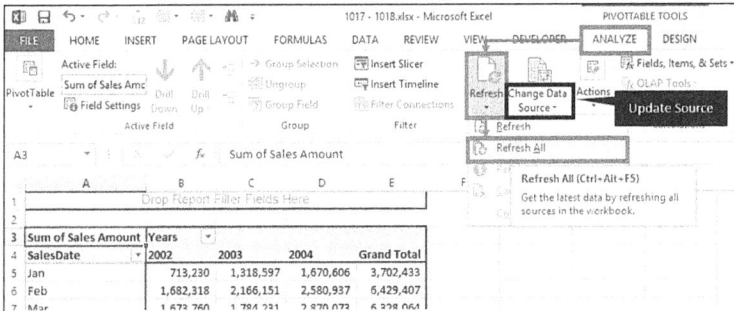

#1012: *Pivot Table—Auto Refresh*

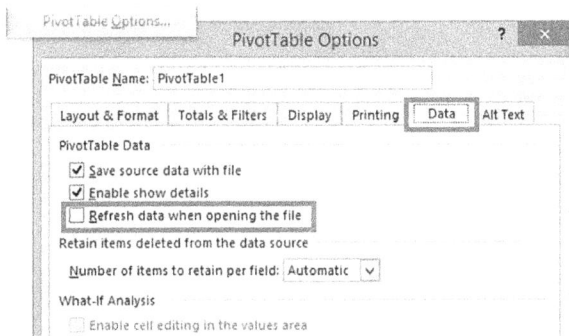

#1013: Pivot Chart Shortcut (F11) and Sparklines

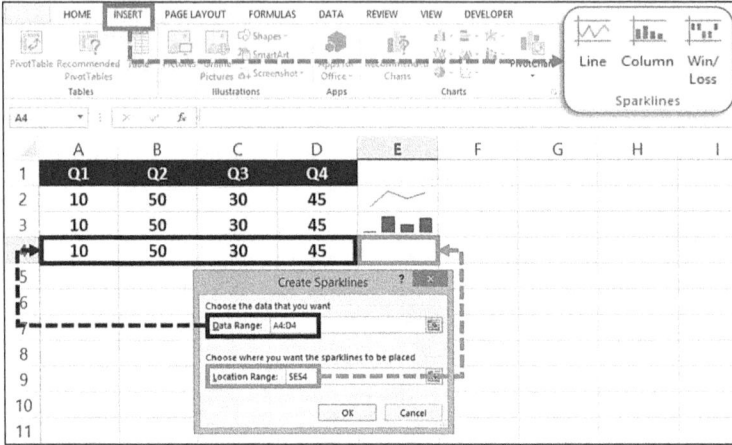

#1014: Pivot Table—Drill Down Option

Double-click on ANY value in the "Value Fields" area where all numbers are displayed to drill-down deeper in the details of the number clicked upon.

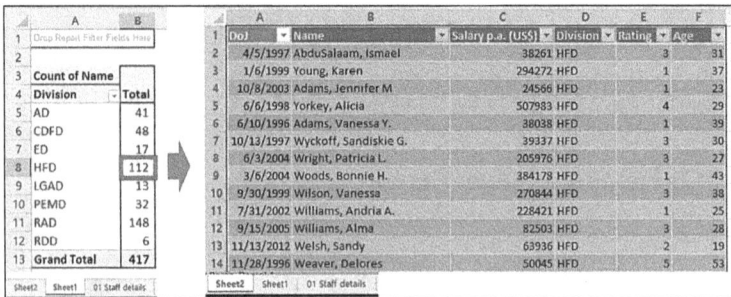

#1015: Report Filter—Generating 100s of Reports in Few Seconds

#1016: Slicer vs. Report Filter

Slicers are easy-to-use filtering components that contain a set of buttons that enable you to quickly filter (single/multiple) the data in a Pivot Table report, without the need to open drop-down lists to find the items that you want to filter.

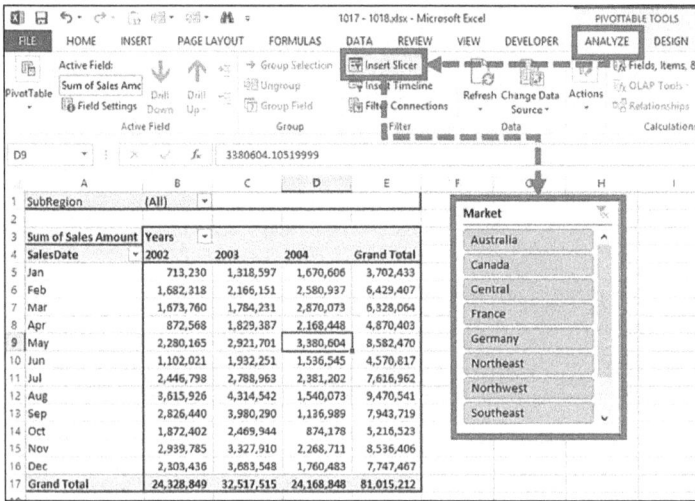

NB: For generating a quick Chart based on Pivot Table report: Select entire Pivot Table report, then Press **<F11>** for generating default chart.

Overview of Lookup Formulas

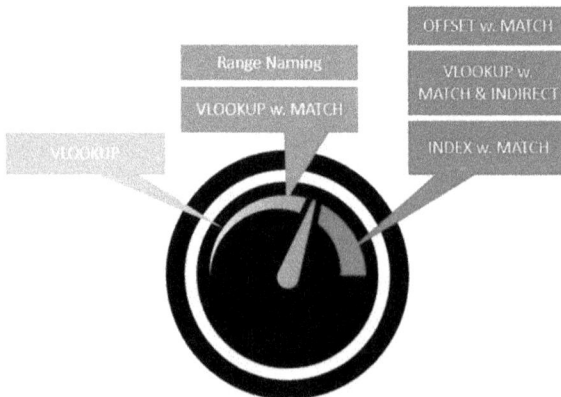

#1101: VLOOKUP() *for Starters*

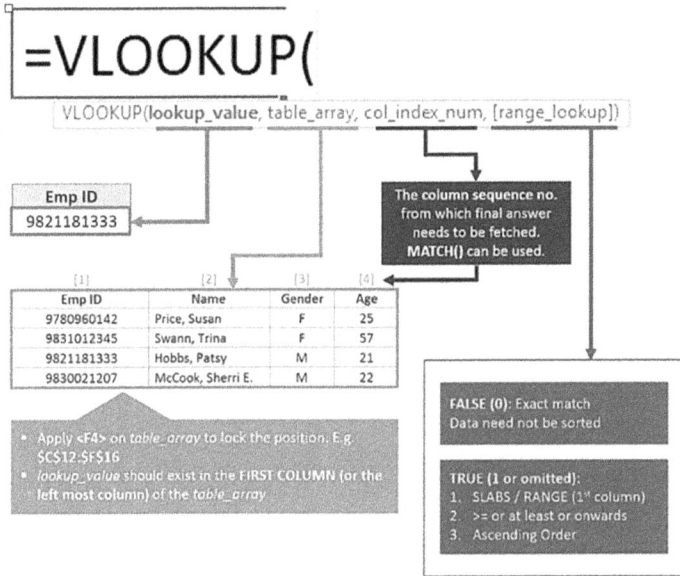

```
=VLOOKUP(
```

VLOOKUP(**lookup_value**, table_array, col_index_num, [range_lookup])

Emp ID
9821181333

The column sequence no. from which final answer needs to be fetched. MATCH() can be used.

	[1]	[2]	[3]	[4]
	Emp ID	Name	Gender	Age
	9780960142	Price, Susan	F	25
	9831012345	Swann, Trina	F	57
	9821181333	Hobbs, Patsy	M	21
	9830021207	McCook, Sherri E.	M	22

FALSE (0): Exact match
Data need not be sorted

- Apply <F4> on *table_array* to lock the position. E.g. $C$12:$F$16
- *lookup_value* should exist in the FIRST COLUMN (or the left most column) of the *table_array*

TRUE (1 or omitted):
1. SLABS / RANGE (1ˢᵗ column)
2. >= or at least or onwards
3. Ascending Order

- "lookup_value" should be in the same format as the one stored in the first column of the selected "table_array."
- Detection techniques: ISNUMBER(), ISTEXT(), LEN().
- Correction techniques for **numbers stored as text**— VALUE(), Text-to-Columns (Step 3/3)—General.
- Right-Click > Format Cells is NA unless <F2 and Enter > on individual cells.

#1102 VLOOKUP w. TRUE vs. FALSE and Applications of TRUE

Three conditions (as applicable for Dates and Number):

- SLABS
- >=
- Ascending Order

Better substitute for complex Nested IFs in significant number of cases. Examples:

GRADING	>=						
	0	Fail		100	Distinction		
	40	Pass		40	Pass		
	90	Distinction		89	Pass		

RENT	>=						
	0	20,000	1	2	3	4	5	6	7
	2	24,000	20,000	24,000	24,000	24,000	30,000	30,000	30,000
	5	30,000						

DEBTORS' AGEING	>=			
	0	0-30	122	91-180
	31	31-60	15	0-30
	61	61-90	76	61-90
	91	91-180	190	>180
	181	>180	54	31-60

Quarter	>=			
	0	Before 2014-15	15-Sep-14	Q2 2014-15
	1-Apr-14	Q1 2014-15	3-Jun-14	Q1 2014-15
	1-Jul-14	Q2 2014-15	1-Jan-16	After 2014-15
	1-Oct-14	Q3 2014-15	4-Dec-11	Before 2014-15
	1-Jan-15	Q4 2014-15		
	1-Apr-15	After 2014-15		

#1104: HLOOKUP() vs. VLOOKUP()

=VLOOKUP(

VLOOKUP(lookup_value, table_array, col_index_num, [range_lookup])

=HLOOKUP(

HLOOKUP(lookup_value, table_array, row_index_num, [range_lookup])

#1105–1106: MATCH()—Basics and Match_Type: -1 vs. 0 vs. 1

	A	B	C	D	E	F	G
1							
2							
3		Black	6				
4							
5		Company name		=MATCH(B3,$B$5:$B$10,0)			
6		Orange		MATCH(lookup_value, lookup_array, [match_type])			
7		Red					
8		Blue					
9		Pink					
10		Black					
11							

[MATCH helps count the **position number** (1st, 2nd, 3rd…) in a **one-dimensional data range**]

MATCH() with 1	MATCH() with -1
▪ Slab	▪ Slab
▪ With values in ascending order	▪ With values in descending order
▪ Greater than equal to (>=)	▪ Less than equal to (<=)

#1107–1111: 2-D Lookup (Vertical + Horizontal)— VLOOKUP w. MATCH

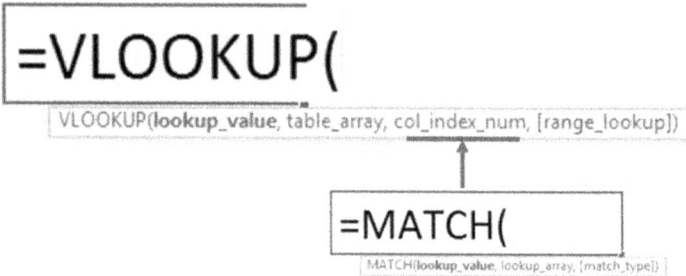

=VLOOKUP(

VLOOKUP(**lookup_value**, table_array, col_index_num, [range_lookup])

=MATCH(

MATCH(**lookup_value**, lookup_array, [match_type])

VLOOKUP()
captures the entire *table_array* and hence, referred as the **SENIOR**

Emp ID	Name	Gender	Age
9780960142	Price, Susan	F	25
9831012345	Swann, Trina	F	57
9821181333	Hobbs, Patsy	M	21
9830021207	McCook, Sherri E.	M	22

MATCH()
captures only the *header* or the *lookup_array* and hence, referred as the **JUNIOR**. It will count the *col_index_number* for VLOOKUP

VLookup + Match is used in dataset with two-variables as placed in the given format. The two defines the answer which is placed inside the table.	

#1112: 2-D Lookup (Horizontal + Vertical)—
HLOOKUP w. MATCH

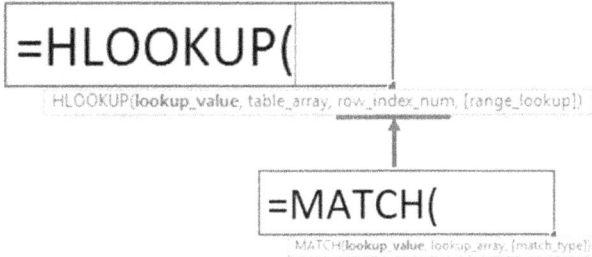

=HLOOKUP(

HLOOKUP(**lookup_value**, table_array, row_index_num, [range_lookup])

=MATCH(

MATCH(**lookup_value**, lookup_array, [match_type])

HLOOKUP()

Emp ID	9780960142	9831012345	9821181333	9830021207
Name	Price, Susan	Swann, Trina	Hobbs, Patsy	McCook, Sherri E.
Gender	F	F	M	M
Age	25	57	21	22

MATCH()

#1113–1114: INDIRECT()—*Basics Along with Range Naming—Applications ["RE-DIRECTION"]*

INDIRECT() w. cell reference	INDIRECT() w. named range
Solution in cell B4 is <u>Blue.</u>	

Note:

- Use INDIRECT when you want to change the reference to a cell within a formula without changing the formula itself.
- Named Cell/Range can be used as an input for INDIRECT.
- Often used to create 3D Lookup formulas along with VLookup + Match.
- INDIRECT() is used for references within the SAME workbook. Cross-linking different workbook is best avoided as it works only when all relevant workbooks are open—Yields a #REF! error if not done so.

Example:

#1115—1116: 3-D Lookup—VLOOKUP() w. MATCH() w. INDIRECT()

=VLOOKUP(F5,INDIRECT(D5),MATCH(C5,INDIRECT(E5),0),0)

Important Note: Using =INDIRECT() with Naming for 3-D Lookup. For example, APAC (Sr.) and APACH (Jr.).

#1117–1119: 3 Reverse Lookup—INDEX() w. MATCH()

IMM vs VM: Both VM and IMM approaches are useful for pulling data from any 2 × 2 data matrix. However, IMM is useful for reverse Lookup. Unlike VM, IMM doesn't require the common link values to be in the left-most column of the database.

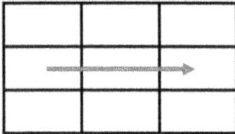

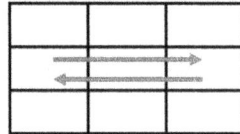

VLOOKUP   **vs.**   **INDEX**

array   row_num   col_num

=INDEX(⬚⬚ , ⬚ , ⬚⬚)

=MATCH(

MATCH(lookup_value, lookup_array, [match_type])

Name	Emp ID	Gender	Age
Price, Susan	9780960142	F	25
Swann, Trina	9831012345	F	57
Hobbs, Patsy	9821181333	M	21
McCook, Sherri E.	9830021207	M	22

#1120–1121: SUMIFS(): Conditional Summation

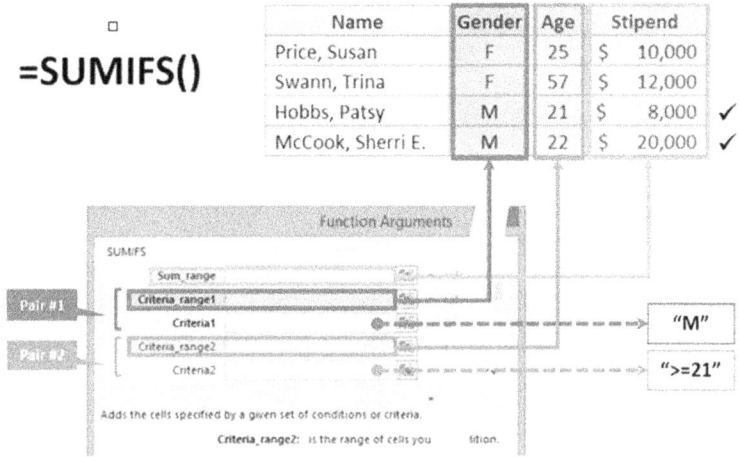

Name	Gender	Age	Stipend	
Price, Susan	F	25	$ 10,000	
Swann, Trina	F	57	$ 12,000	
Hobbs, Patsy	M	21	$ 8,000	✓
McCook, Sherri E.	M	22	$ 20,000	✓

- Solution: 28,000

Note:

1. Use <F4> to lock *Criteria_range* and *Sum_range*.
2. Maintain SAME HEIGHT of RANGES.
3. SUMIFS can accept multiple criteria (127!) whereas SUMIF can accept only one.

#1122: SUMIFS(): Conditional Summation (Three Criteria) w. Date Range

- If Cell A1 contains "21-May-2001," then the *Criteria_1* can be **">="&A1** indicating date 21-May-2001 onwards. The operators (> < = etc.) has to be enclosed in a pair of double-quotes and concatenated (&) with the cell reference containing valid date(s).

#1123: SUMIFS(): Condition-Based Selective Cumulative Running Total

```
=SUMIFS($C$1:C1,$B$1:B1,A1)
```

SUMIFS(sum_range, criteria_range1, criteria1, [criteria_range2, criteria2], ...)

- Careful use of relative references ($) can help yield **differential cumulative running total.**

#1124: COUNTIFS()—Single/Multiple Criteria: Duplicate Count, Instance No.

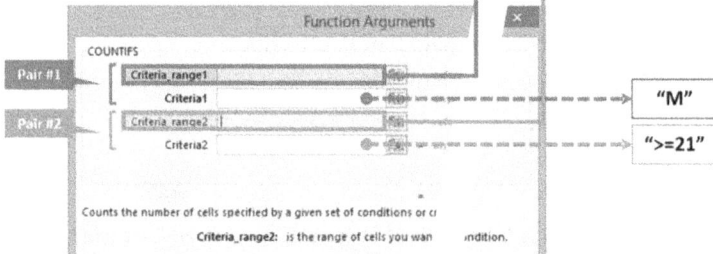

=COUNTIFS()

Name	Gender	Age	Stipend	
Price, Susan	F	25	$ 10,000	
Swann, Trina	F	57	$ 12,000	
Hobbs, Patsy	M	21	$ 8,000	✓
McCook, Sherri E.	M	22	$ 20,000	✓

- Solution: 2
- Used for 2-way list-reconciliation, duplicate count.
  For example, **=COUNTIFS($A$1:$A$100,A1).**
- Used for Instance No./Occurrence No.
  =COUNTIFS($A$1:A1,A1).

#1201–1206: *Text Formulas: UPPER(), PROPER() and LOWER(); TRIM(), VALUE(), T(), N(), REPT()*

=PROPER(PROPER(text)	• Capitalizes the **first letter in each word** of a text value. • For example, converts **"the man eats"** or **"THE MAN EATS"** TO **"The Man Eats."**
=UPPER(UPPER(text)	• Converts text to uppercase. • For example, converts **"the man eats"** or **"The Man Eats"** TO **"THE MAN EATS."**
=LOWER(LOWER(text)	• Converts text to lowercase. • For example,, converts **"The Man Eats"** or **"THE MAN EATS"** TO **"the man eats."**
=TRIM(TRIM(text)	• Removes excess spaces from text. Removes all leading and trailing spaces. However, multiple spaces inside the sentences are replaced with a single space. • For example, converts " **HSBC Inc.**" TO "**HSBC Inc.**"
=LEN(LEN(text)	• Returns the number of characters in a text string. • For example, AK 47 =LEN(___) = 5
=VALUE(VALUE(text)	• Converts "a number stored as text" to a number. • "A number stored as text" is recognized as 0 for computations.
=T(T(value)	• If value is or refers to text, T returns value. If value does not refer to text, T returns "" (empty text).
=N(N(value)	• Converts a value to a number in Excel. For text, it yields zero. • Used to leave in-cell comments. For example, =SUM(B1:B2) + N("This is my comment—Hello World").
=REPT(REPT(text, number_times)	• Repeats a string/character specified number of times. • For example, =REPT("X,"3) will yield XXX.

#1207: *Joining Data Strings Using* CONCATENATE, &

	A	B	C	D	E
1					
2	AK7	2332	AK7-2332	=A2&"-"&B2	
3					
4	AK7	2332	AK7-2332	=CONCATENATE(A4,"-",B4)	

Note:

- Both of the above approaches yield the SAME output.
- Any external text, number, symbol must be enclosed in a pair of double quotations. For example, " "
- =TEXT() may be used if combining Dates. For example, ="Today's date is" & TEXT(A2,"dd-mmm-yy")

#1208–1209: *Find & Replace*

Basics

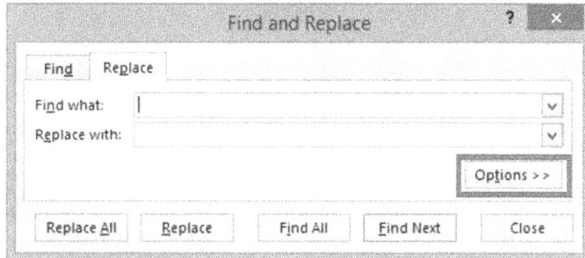

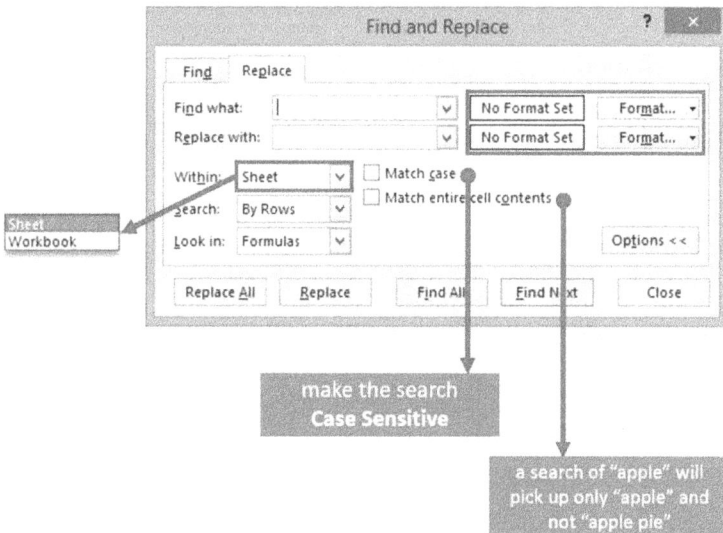

Using Wildcard Characters (*?)

*	Asterisk (*): Any number of characters

Using Wildcard Characters (*?)

?	Question (?): Any one character (single)

#1210: Find and Replace—Neutralizing Wildcard Characters to Remove Them from Data

Important: Wildcard characters can be neutralized by prefixing tilde sign (~) which is placed above the TAB key:

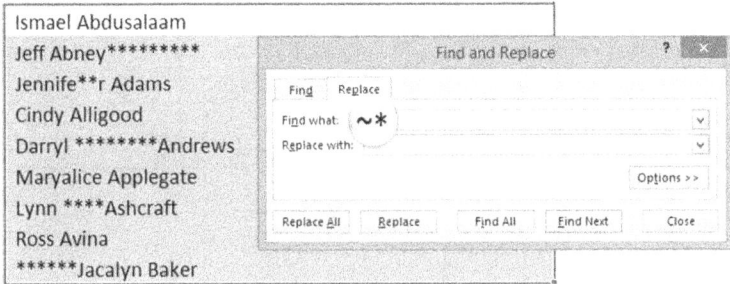

#1211: Find & Replace—Word vs. Excel

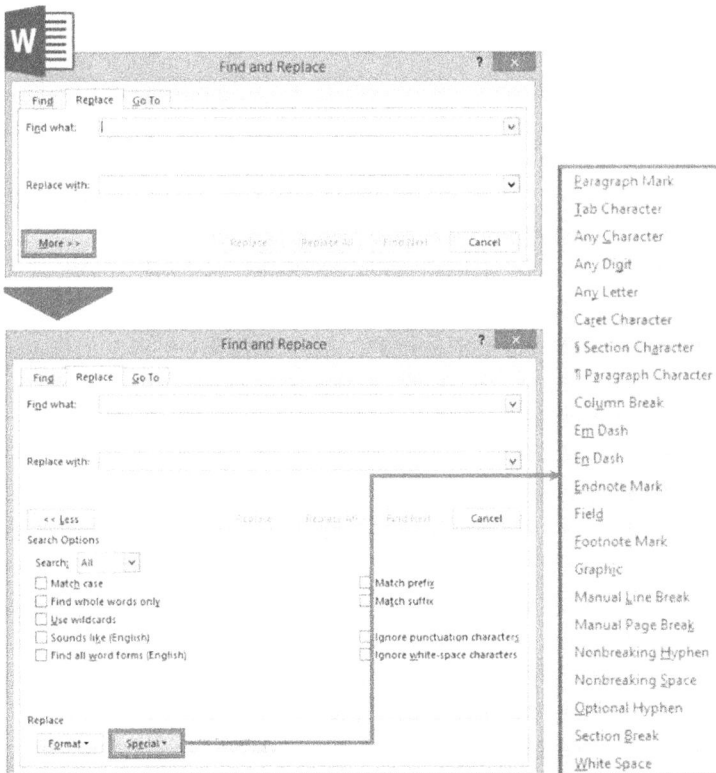

#1212: Find and Replace—Cell Format

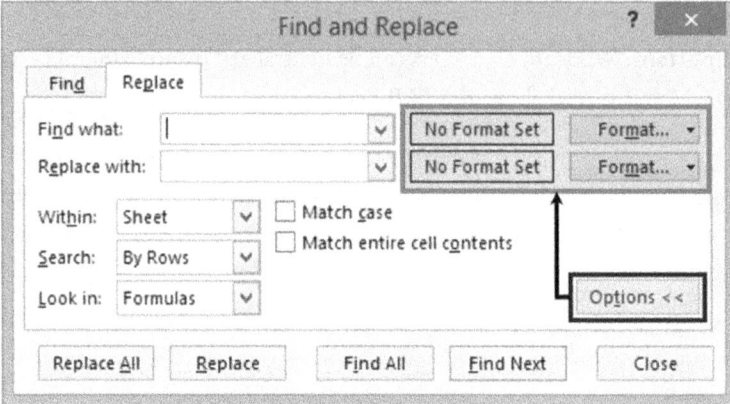

- FIND WHAT: Specify the **source** format.
- REPLACE WITH: Specify the **target** format.

#1213–1214: Text to Columns—Delimited vs. Fixed Width

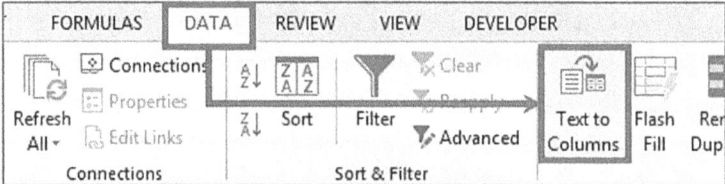

#1214: Text to Columns—Tricks

Trick 1: Ensuring a predefined format for exported data @ Step 3 of 3. Applications: Numbers stored as text to General format—refer VLookup discussion.

- Dates cleaning.
- Retaining prefix zeroes in cases of credit card and bank account numbers, ID codes.

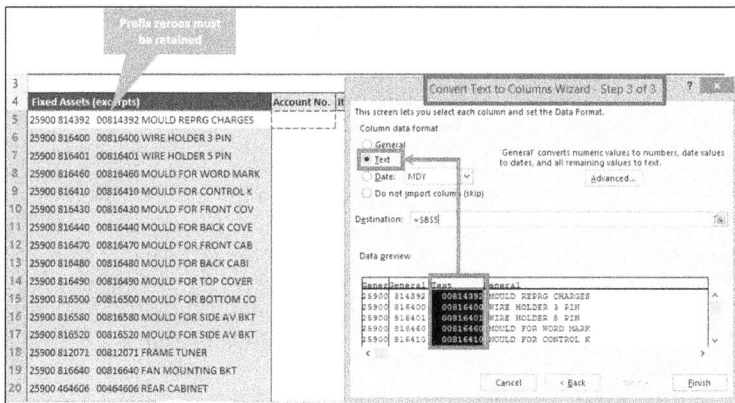

- For keeping intact a number string with zeroes at the begin- ning (prefix): In Step 3 of 3, select the relevant "Column" under "Data preview" section Ú Column will blacken out Ú Choose Text radio button to store the output column in text form.

#1215–1216: Text to Columns—Cleaning up Numbers w. Trailing Minus Sign; Replacing Dr/Cr w. +/-

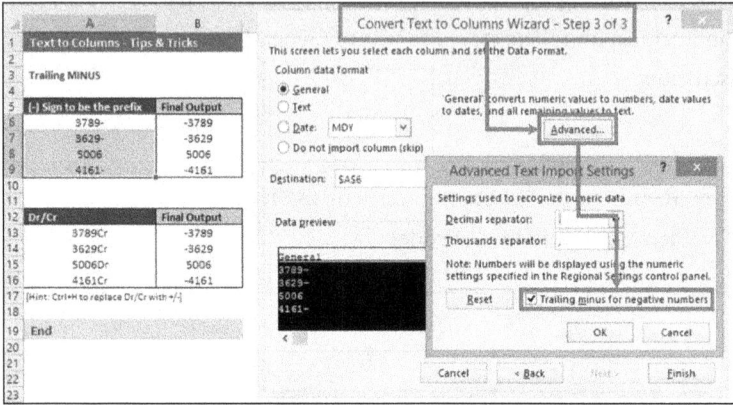

- Text to Columns is also used to rectify numbers with **trailing negative (-) sign**s. For example, from 212- to -212.

#1217–1218: Text to Columns—Correcting Invalid Dates

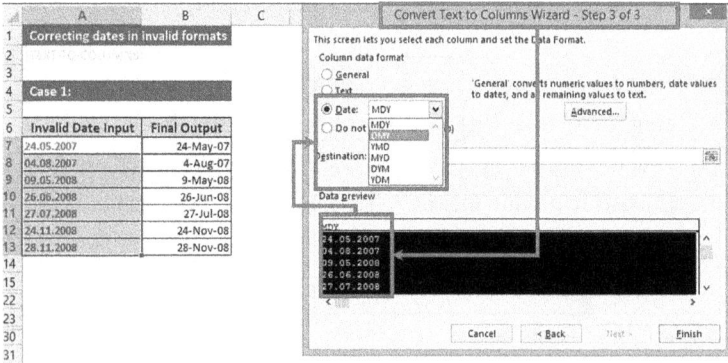

- **For Correcting Dates**—Apply "*Confession Box.*" Choose the mistake or the current sequence of date components
- For example, "DMY"—29.10.2009 and "YMD" for 20091031.

#1219–1221: LEFT(), RIGHT(), MID()

=LEFT(LEFT(text, [num_chars])	• Extract specified number of characters from left, right, or mid.
=RIGHT(RIGHT(text, [num_chars])	
=MID(MID(text, start_num, num_chars)	

	A	B	C
1	AJCPP1312N	AJ	=LEFT(A1,2)
2	AJCPP1312N	2N	=RIGHT(A2,2)
3	AJCPP1312N	P	=MID(A3,4,1)

=LEN
fx LEN   Returns the number of characters in a text string

• "characters" includes space

#1219–1221: SEARCH() vs. FIND()

• Yield the starting position of the criteria.

=SEARCH(SEARCH(find_text, within_text, [start_num])	• Case Sensitive?—No • Can use wild characters in search terms?—Yes
=FIND(FIND(find_text, within_text, [start_num])	• Case Sensitive?—Yes • Can use wild characters in search terms?—No

	A	B	C
1	user@yodalearning.com	6	=SEARCH("YO*",A1)
2	123456........................21		

#1301: Lowgical Formulas—Generally Used with IF()

=ISBLANK
fx ISBLANK   Checks whether a reference is to an empty cell, and returns TRUE or FALSE

=ISNUMBER
fx ISNUMBER   Checks whether a value is a number, and returns TRUE or FALSE

[Used to check the validity of dates as technically every valid date in Excel is a "number."]

=ISTEXT
fx ISTEXT   Checks whether a value is text, and returns TRUE or FALSE

=ISERROR
fx ISERROR   Checks whether a value is an error (#N/A, #VALUE!, #REF!, #DIV/0!, #NUM!, #NAME?, or #NULL!), and return TRUE or FALSE

=ISFORMULA
fx ISFORMULA   Checks whether a reference is to a cell containing a formula, and returns TRUE or FALSE

Others: ISNA(), ISREF(), ISERR()

#1302–1304: Logical Formulas—AND(), OR(), IF()

```
=AND
      [AND]  Checks whether all arguments are TRUE, and returns TRUE if all arguments are TRUE
```

```
=OR
      [OR]  Checks whether any of the arguments are TRUE, and returns TRUE or FALSE. Returns FALSE only if all arguments are FALSE
```

```
=IF(
      IF(logical_test, [value_if_true], [value_if_false])
```

Examples:

	A	B	C	D	E	G
8	Name	Salary p.a. (US$)	Division	Rating	Rating 1-3 AND Division "CDFD" AND Salary < 50K	
9	AbduSalaam, Ismael	38,261	HFD	3	=AND(D9<4,C9="CDFD",B9<50000)	
426					AND(logical1, [logical2], [logical3], [logical4], ...)	

[FALSE because Division is not equal to "CDFD."]

	A	B	C	D	F	G
8	Name	Salary p.a. (US$)	Division	Rating	Rating 1-3 AND Division "CDFD" AND Salary < 50K	
9	AbduSalaam, Ismael	38,261	HFD	3	=OR(D9<4,C9="CDFD",B9<50000)	
426					OR(logical1, [logical2], [logical3], [logical4], ...)	

[TRUE because at least one of three conditions is TRUE.]

	A	B	C	D	F	G	H	I
8	Name	Salary p.a. (US$)	Division	Rating	Rating 1-3 AND Division "CDFD" AND Salary < 50K			
9	AbduSalaam, Ismael	38,261	HFD	3	=IF(OR(D9<4,C9="CDFD",B9<50000),"Bonus","No Bonus")			

[Bonus.]

=IFERROR(IFERROR(value, value_if_error)	▪ =IFERROR(VLOOKUP(), "Data Not Available") ▪ =IFERROR(VLOOKUP(), IFERROR(VLOOKUP(), "Data Not Available")) ▪ =IFERROR(VLOOKUP(), VLOOKUP())
▪ Prior to v. 2007 that is, before IFERROR() was introduced, users used =IF(ISERROR(VLOOKUP()), VLOOKUP(), "Data Not Available") instead of =IFERROR(VLOOKUP(), "Data Not Available")	

	A	B	§ C	▪ Not equal is referred by <>.
1	2		2 =A1<>B1	▪ Answer = FALSE.

#1401–1403: Conditional Formatting

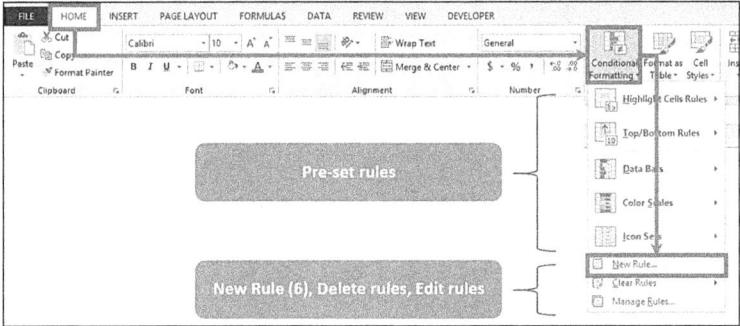

Manage Rules

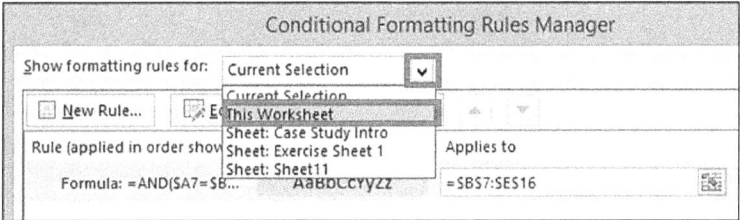

#1403: Conditional Formatting: Data Bars, Color Scales, Icon Sets

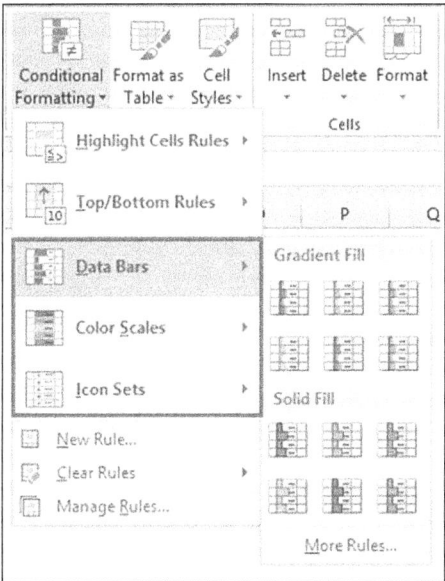

#1404: *Conditional Formatting: Blanks, Errors, Values, Duplicates*

Most commonly used "Rule":

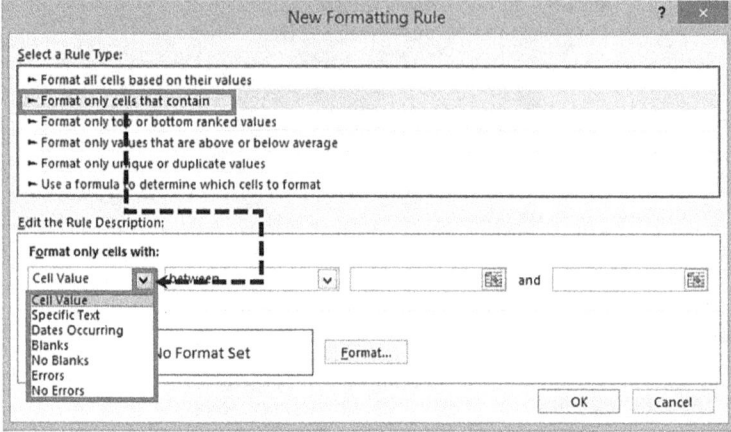

#1405–1407: *Conditional Formatting: Formula Based*

Important:

- Formula should yield TRUE or FALSE as an answer.
- Relative references ($). For example, $C8.
- Formula in line with selection of data range. For example, $C8 because selection of data range starts from the 8th row.

#1501: *Activating Developer Tab in v. 2007*
OFFICE BUTTON > EXCEL OPTIONS

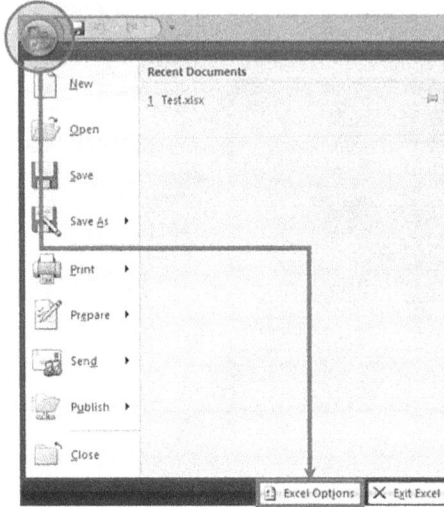

POPULAR > Show Developer tab in the Ribbon

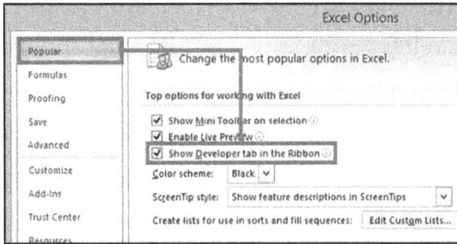

#1501: *Activating Developer Tab in v. 2010–13*

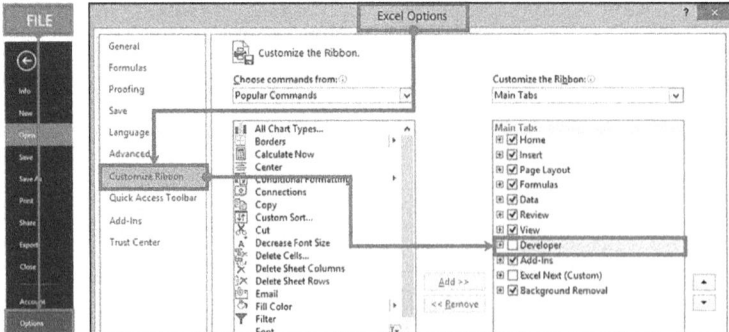

#1501–1502: *Using Form Control Buttons from Developer Tab (Spin Bar, Scroll Bar) + Limitations*

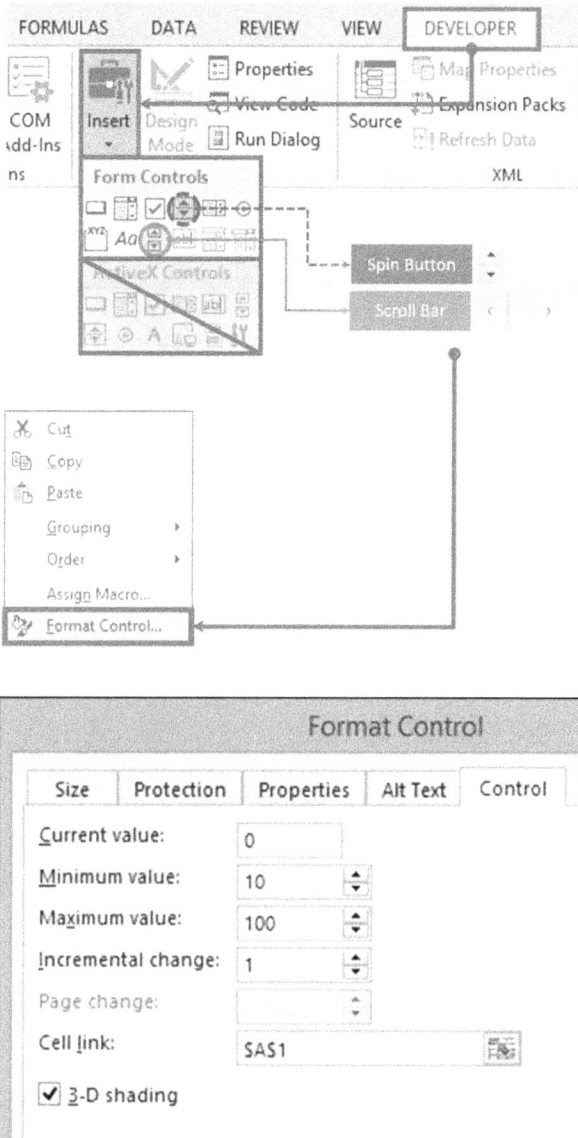

NB: The feature is used to change the input values (assumptions) at the click of a button. The referred "Form Control" buttons cannot accommodate <u>decimal values</u>, <u>% values</u> or a value <u>outside 0-30,000 range</u>.

#1504: PMT

=PMT()

Function Arguments			
Rate	10%/12	=	0.008333333
Nper	36	=	36
Pv	750000	=	750000
Fv		=	number
Type	0	=	0
		=	-24200.3904 ← EMI

Calculates the payment for a loan based on constant payments and a constant interest rate.

Type is a logical value: payment at the beginning of the period = 1; payment at the end of the period = 0 or omitted.

Formula result = -24200.3904

Help on this function   OK   Cancel

#1504: What IF Analysis—Goal Seek

Goal Seek helps back calculate input based on predefined target answer.

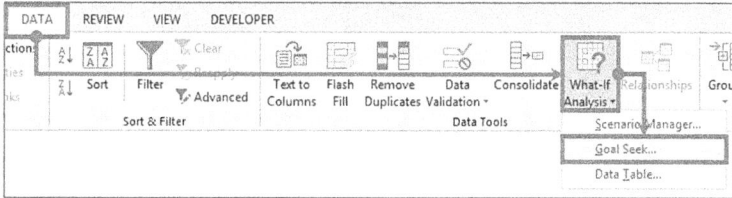

Here it's targeting an EMI of Rs. 20,000 and is trying to back calculate what can be the loan amount given the fixed duration and interest %.

	A	B	C	D
1				
2	Loan Amt. Rs.	500,000.0	Goal Seek	
3	Interest % p.a.	13.0%	Set cell: $B$7	
4	Duration (Yrs.)	2.0	To value: -20000	
5			By changing cell: $B$2	
6			OK Cancel	
7	EMI (Rs.) using PMT	(23,771)		
8		=PMT(B3/12,B4*12,B2)		

	A	B
1		
2	Loan Amt. Rs.	420,682.2
3	Interest % p.a.	13.0%
4	Duration (Yrs.)	2.0
5		
6		
7	EMI (Rs.) using PMT	(20,000)
8		=PMT(B3/12,B4*12,B2)

#1505–1506: What IF Analysis—Data Tables (Sensitivity Analysis)

Price and Quantity leads to revenue. Cost component includes Fixed and Variable component. Comparing Revenue vs. Cost yields Profit.

A	B	C
1	DATA TABLES	
2		
3	Sample Revenue-Cost Model	
4		
5	Price (Rs.)	15.00
6	Quantity sold	2,000
7	Revenue	30,000
8		
9	Variable Cost (Cost of Material, Labor)	15,000
10	Fixed Cost (Rent, Salary etc)	20,000
11	Total Cost	35,000
12		
13	Profit= Revenue less Total Cost	(5,000)
14		
15		
16	Assumption: Variable cost as a % of Revenue	50.0

Step 1: Set the layout with up to two variables.

A	E	F	G	H	I	J
1						
2						
3		1500	2000	2500	3000	3500
4	10					
5	=E4+1			Qty Sold		
6	12					
7	13					
8	14					
9	15	Price				
10						

Step 2: At the intersection of the two-variables (top-left of the table), point the cell to the cell containing formula for effect value. For example, C13 refers to Profit.

Step 3: Choose the table area (not more not less).

Step 4: Go to "Data Table."

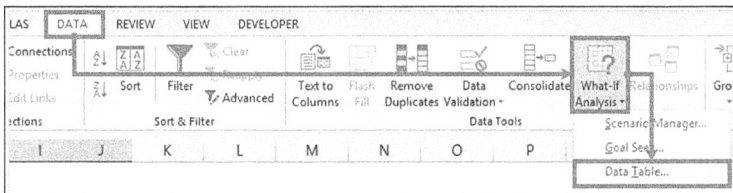

Step 4: Row Input Cell and Column Input Cell (single cell reference each).

	A	B	C	D	E	F	G	H	I	J
1	DATA TABLES									
2										
3		Sample Revenue-Cost Model				(5,000)	1500	2000	2500	3000	3500
4						10					
5		Price (Rs.)	15.00			11					
6		Quantity sold	2,000			12		Data Table	?		
7		Revenue	30,000			13		Row input cell $C$6			
8						14		Column input cell $C$5			
9		Variable Cost (Cost of Material, Labor)	15,000			15		OK	Cancel		
10		Fixed Cost (Rent, Salary etc)	20,000								
11		Total Cost	35,000								
12											
13		Profit= Revenue less Total Cost	(5,000)								
14											
15											
16		Assumption: Variable cost as a % of Revenue	50.0								
17											

VC	Vertical data (Say Prices)	Column Input Cell ($C$5)
HR	Horizontal data (say Qty Sold)	Row Input Cell ($C$6)

Result: Generated Output—two-variable sensitivity analysis

	A	E	F	G	H	I	J
1							
2							
	Impact on Profit due to changes in Price & Qty	(5,000)	1500	2000	2500	3000	3500
		10	-12500	-10000	-7500	-5000	-2500
		11	-11750	-9000	-6250	-3500	-750
		12	-11000	-8000	-5000	-2000	1000
7		13	-10250	-7000	-3750	-500	2750
8		14	-9500	-6000	-2500	1000	4500
9		15	-8750	-5000	-1250	2500	6250
10							

NB: Conditional Formatting can be applied to apply green/red colors for positive/negative numbers.

#1507–1508: Data Tables (Sensitivity Analysis)—Two Inputs and multiple Output

Step 1: Drop-Down list.

Step 2: Output cells "named" using Name Box—same names used as list values of drop-down.

Step 3: Using INDIRECT() in the Data Table—pointing to the cell containing drop-down list.

	A	E	F	G	H	I	J
1		Revenue					
2							
3		=INDIRECT(E1)		2000	2500	3000	3500
4		INDIRECT(ref_text, [a1])	20000	25000	30000	35000
5		11	16500	22000	27500	33000	38500
6		12	18000	24000	30000	36000	42000
7		13	19500	26000	32500	39000	45500
8		14	21000	28000	35000	42000	49000
9		15	22500	30000	37500	45000	52500
10							

NB: Form Control Buttons (Developer > Insert > Form Controls) can applied to control input numbers.

#1601–1604A: Category-Wise SubTotal with Groupings

Supplier Names have been "Grouped" in clusters along with a "Subtotal" at the end of the list.

Step 1: SORT the dataset with respect to the column heading on whose basis the Subtotal shall be generated. For example, Supplier Name.

Step 2: DATA tab > SUBTOTAL.

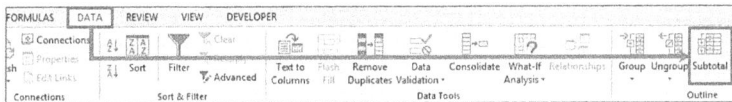

Step 3:

1. Choose the column name which has been sorted.
2. SUM, MAX, AVERAGE, and so on.
3. Choose column(s) under which Subtotal is needed.
4. For multilevel Subtotal, multilevel SORT is needed. Plus, tick away "Replace current subtotals."
5. For removing Subtotal, select entire dataset and use "Remove All" button (bottom-left) from the Subtotal main box.

NB: Use <Ctrl + G> - Visible Cells to highlight subtotal rows [Shortcut—ALT;].

#1605–1606: Consolidate - Two and Three Dimensions

1. Function to be used for Consolidation: SUM, MAX, MIN, AVERAGE, and so on.
2. Source of data should be selected and "added."
3. Required for "Labels" and "Links to Source data."

Result:

#1701–1702: Cell Level Security

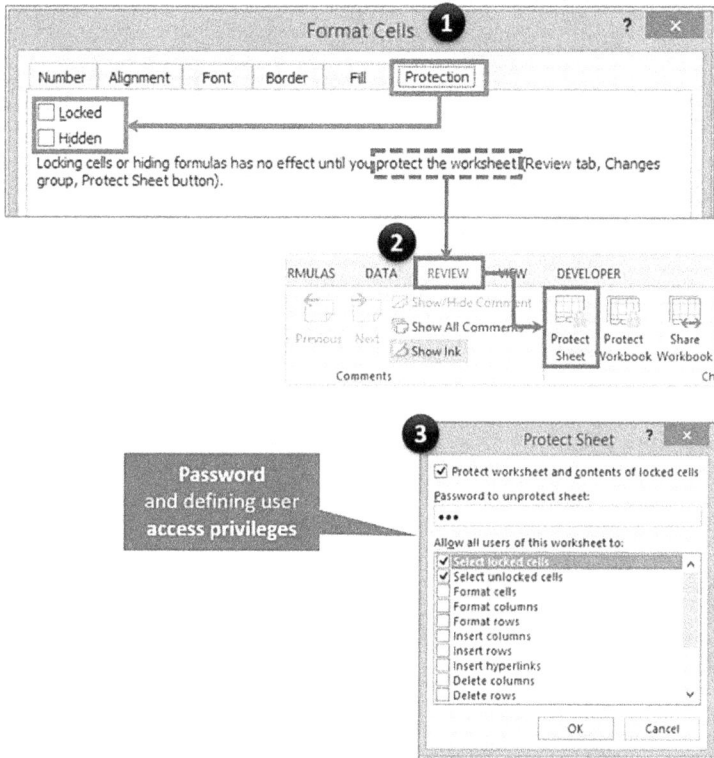

Note: By default, ALL cells are "Locked" (identified for protection). Ensure that ALL cells in the sheet are "Unlocked" and only chosen ones are "Locked." Else ALL cells will be locked and no changes can be made.

$703: Sheet Level Security [Protect Workbook Structure]

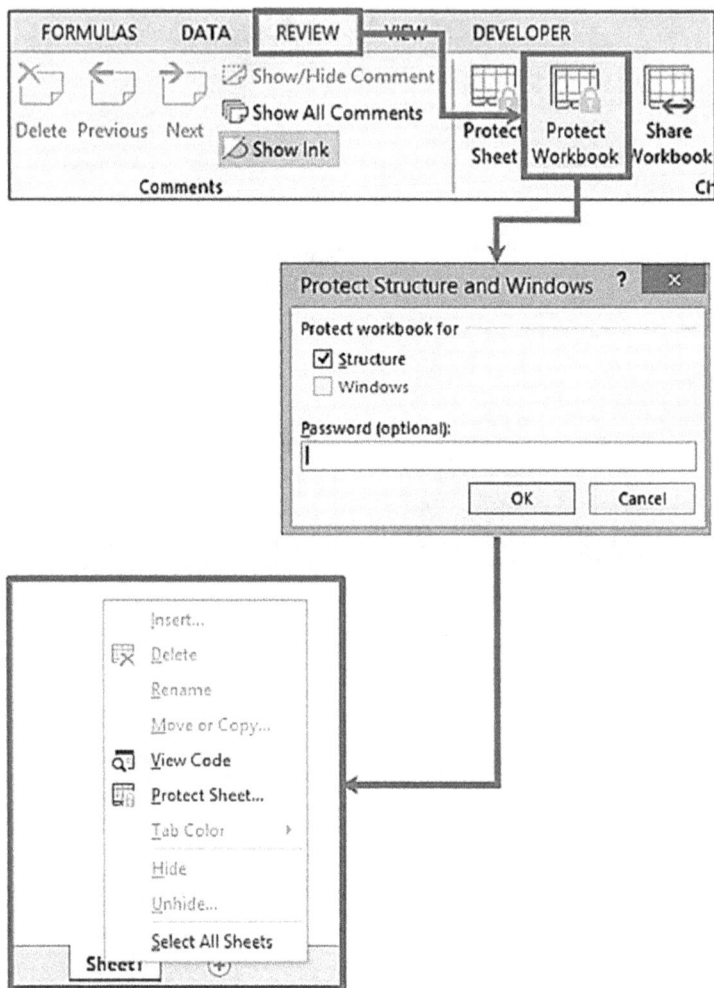

#703: Sheet Level Security [Sheet Properties—"Very Hidden"]

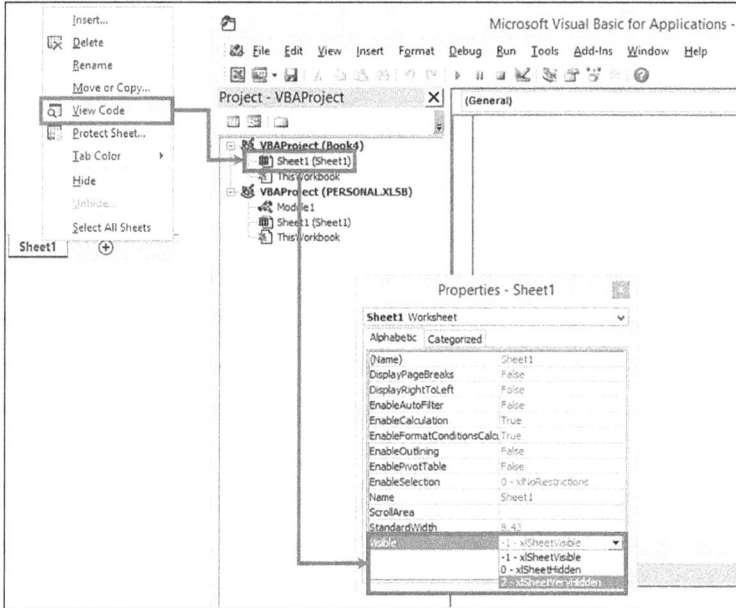

#704: File Level Security

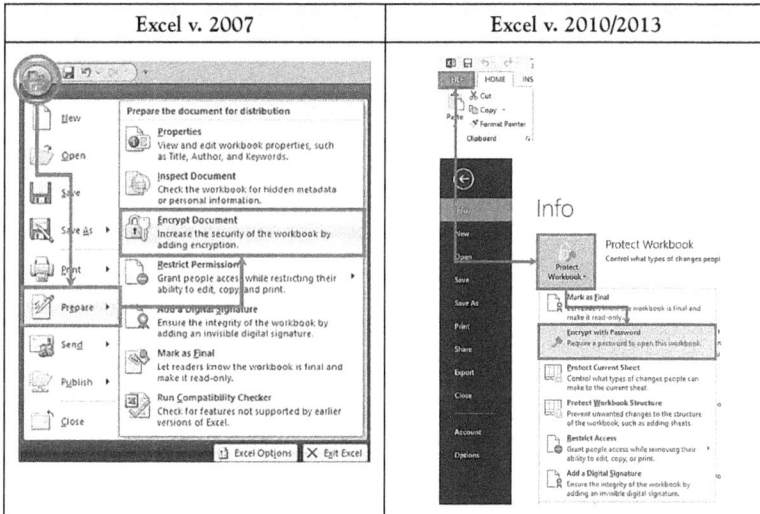

#1801: *Page Set Up*

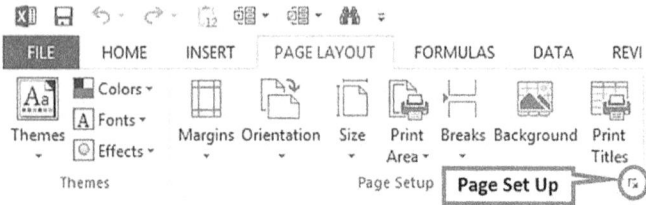

SN	Shortcut Key/Path	Objective
1	ALT, P, S, P	Page Set Up
2	CTRL + F2	Print Preview

#1801, 1802, 1804: *Print Tricks*

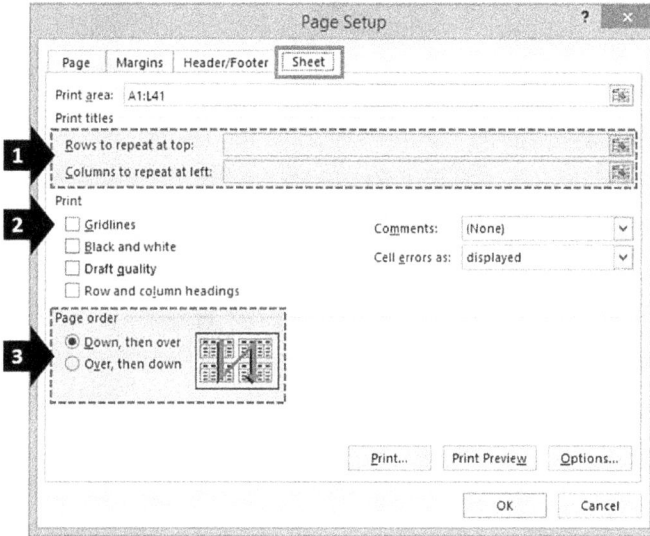

1	Rows to repeat at top	For headers to appear on every page print out. For example, ID, Name, Description, Amount.
2	Gridlines	Switches on/off the dotted-cell border while printing.
3	Page Order—Vertical vs. Horizontal	For worksheets with print area extending to multiple pages—both horizontally and vertically, users can decide the page order of print out.

#1805—1806: Print Tricks for Financial Analysts—Check Underlying Formulas

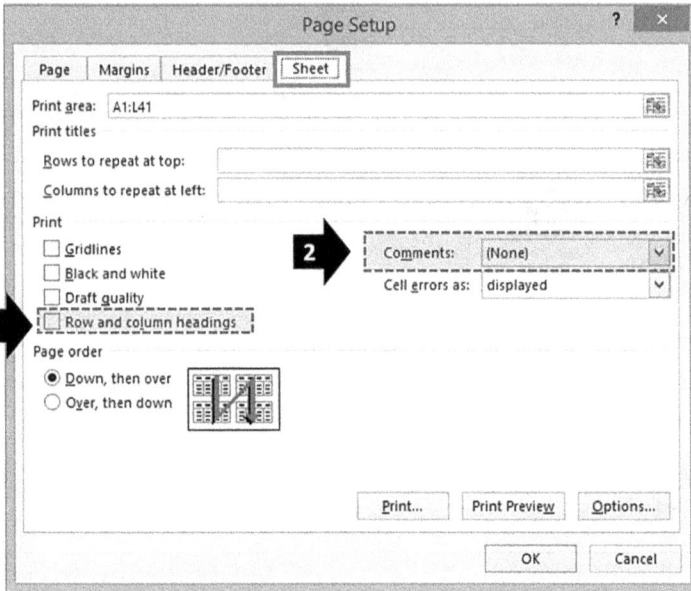

1	Row and Column headings	Displays the row headings (1, 2, 3...) and column headings (A, B, C...) in the print out. To be used after activating the below mentioned shortcut key: • Ctrl` (the special character key above the TAB key)— Displays all formulas of the worksheet.

Audit Trick: Press <u>Ctrl`</u> to "Show all formulas" and then "Print" with "Row and Column headings."

	A	B	C	D
1				
2	CAB Pvt		Reported	Reported
3	Financi:		39538	39903
4				
5				
6	Assump			
7		Sales growth	NA	0.05
8		Costs as % of Sales	=C12/C11	=D12/D11
9				
10	Income			
11		Sales (A)	1201	780
12		Costs (B)	802	511
13		Profit (C=A-B)	=C11-C12	=D11-D12
14				
15		Profit as % of Sales (C/A)	=C13/C11	=D13/D11
16				

2	Comments	Entire worksheet's comments can be displayed at the end of the worksheet along with cell reference. Useful to keep a track of all the in-cell comments that are scattered on the worksheet.

Cell: C8
Comment: Roy Jr.:
    Refer email dtd 21-Apr-2009

Cell: E11
Comment: Yoda Learning:
    Annual Report Pg 21

#1807: *Print Entire Workbook*

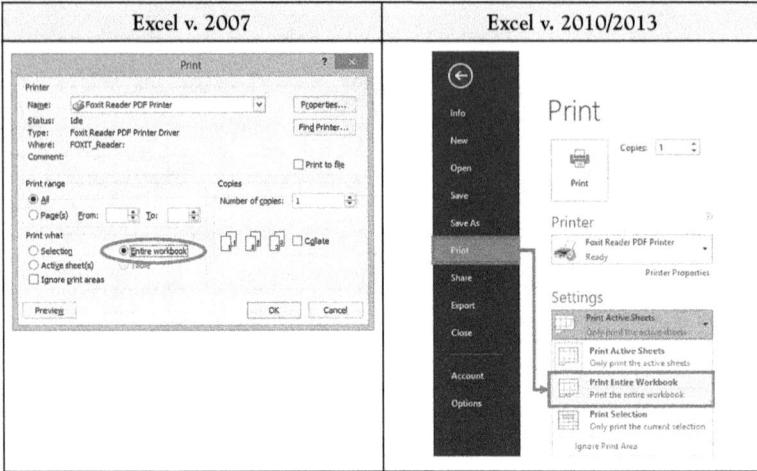

Excel v. 2007	Excel v. 2010/2013

#1901: *Comments—Shortcuts, Inserting Picture in Comment Box*

SN	Shortcut Key/Path	Objective
1	Shift + F2	Insert/Edit Comment
2	ALT, R, A	Show All Comment
3	Ctrl + Shift + O	Go To (Special) -> Comment
4	Ctrl + Alt + V -> Comment	Paste Special -> Comment

Inserting a Picture in the Comment Box

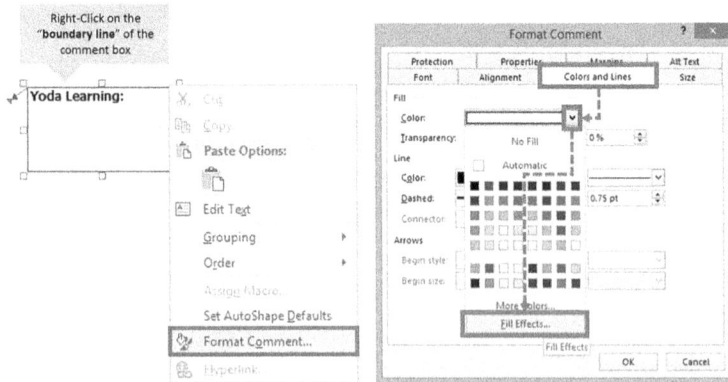

#1902: *Split Windows, Viewing multiple Windows—Simultaneously Working with Different Workbooks, Worksheets and Scattered Cell Ranges Simultaneously*

1	NEW WINDOW	Opens another instance (window) of the active workbook, thus, allowing you to work on different worksheets of the same/different workbook simultaneously. "*Arrange All*" feature will help arrange the open windows side-by-side (horizontal/ vertical).
	Book1:2 - Microsoft Excel	This is how the names of the two instances of the workbook (Book1) will be displayed--Book1:1 and Book1:2

2	ARRANGE ALL	Helps stack/arrange open windows side-by-side
		Important: If multiple workbooks are open and you wish to stack "*windows*" of a specific workbook side-by-side, use the last check-box—"*Windows of active workbook.*" If not chosen, the "*Arrange Windows*" feature will stack **ALL** the windows of all open workbook side-by-side thus, creating a temporary screen clutter.

3	SPLIT	Divides/"Splits" the window into different panes that each scroll differently. It is ideal if you want to work simultaneously on different areas of the SAME worksheet of the workbook. Unlike "*New Window*," it doesn't allow you to work on different worksheets of the same workbook simultaneously.

#1903: Hyperlinking (Ctrl + K)

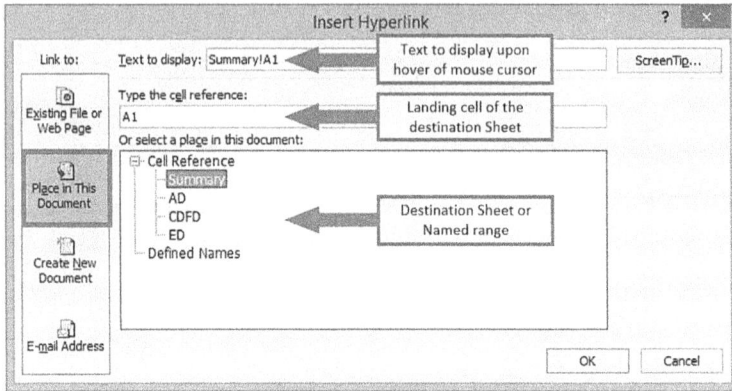

Quick Tip: New Function in v. 2013

=HYPERLINK(	▪ Example: =HYPERLINK("http://cajobportal.com," "Click here for Excel Tricks"). ▪ For more details, refer Microsoft Excel help.
HYPERLINK(link_location, [friendly_name])	

Index